ANNE BRADSTREET

ANNE BRADSTREET

*A Guided Tour of the Life and
Thought of a Puritan Poet*

HEIDI L. NICHOLS

P U B L I S H I N G
P.O. BOX 817 • PHILLIPSBURG • NEW JERSEY 08865-0817

Stained glass image of Anne Bradstreet used by kind permission of the Vicar and Churchwardens of St. Botolph's Church, Boston, England.

Title page of 1678 edition of *The Tenth Muse* courtesy of the Rare Book Division of the Library of Congress.

Page design by Lakeside Design Plus
Typesetting by Dawn Premako

Printed in the United States of America

Library of Congress Cataloging-in-Publication Data

Nichols, Heidi L., 1970–

    Anne Bradstreet : a guided tour of the life and thought of a Puritan poet / Heidi L. Nichols.
       p. cm.
    Includes bibliographical references (p.) and index.
    ISBN-13: 978-0-87552-610-2 (pbk.)
    ISBN-10: 0-87552-610-1 (pbk.)
    1. Bradstreet, Anne, 1612?–1672. 2. Women and literature—New England—History—17th century. 3. Poets, American—Colonial period, ca. 1600–1775—Biography. 4. New England—Intellectual life—17th century. 5. Puritan women—New England—Biography. 6. Puritans—New England—Biography. I. Title.

PS712.N53 2006
811'.1—dc22
[B]

                         2005052130

For My Loving Parents,
Keith and Beverly Haselhorst

CONTENTS

ILLUSTRATIONS

ACKNOWLEDGMENTS

The support of others has enabled me to find the time, energy, and materials necessary to introduce and edit the work of Anne Bradstreet. I offer thanks to the faculty concerns committee at Lancaster Bible College for its support of the project and to the librarians at Lancaster Bible College for interlibrary loan materials. Thanks also go to Charles Hambrick-Stowe for his kind consultation on the initial concept. With two young children of my own—far fewer than Bradstreet's eight, but busy nonetheless—I thank my dear and loving husband, Steve, for making time for me to complete this volume and for offering insightful suggestions throughout. And, I thank my parents, Keith and Beverly Haselhorst, for their never-ending encouragement of me and my studies—and for letting me leave the light on at night to enjoy just one more chapter. It is to them that I dedicate this volume.

INTRODUCTION: WHY READ ANNE BRADSTREET?

She labored poetically on the edge of a wilderness, a vast landscape filled with menacing animals, sometimes hostile Native Americans, and the searing heat and plummeting cold of a harsh New England climate. She resided in a community centered on and governed by religious beliefs. She survived in a time when disease and sickness took a much greater toll than they do today. Perhaps it seems quaint, perhaps spiritual and even intellectual, to read the work of this Puritan woman who wrote nearly four hundred years ago. But with such differences in experience and context, what could she possibly have to say to us?

We can answer this question with typical arguments for reading bygone writers. A study of Anne Bradstreet and her work helps to flesh out the historical record. As a settler in the Massachusetts Bay Colony and as the daughter and wife of two of the colony's early governors, Bradstreet offers insights into the makings and birth pains of this young Puritan colony, as well as into its embattled mother country. Bradstreet's life and work, revealing her vibrant intellectualism and her outspoken love for her husband, challenge stereotypes many still have of the Puritans. And, as an orthodox Puritan, Bradstreet adds another dimension to the study of women in church history, for she differs from the more commonly considered mystical figures of Teresa of Avila and Margery Kempe.

Of course, Bradstreet also deserves reading for literary reasons. She is worthy of exploration simply due to her title as the first published American poet. Once drawn to Bradstreet by such a distinction, the reader is sure to continue to explore both her more formal poetry and her personal lyrics, rich in intellectual and aesthetic rigor and worthy of emulation by the aspiring writer.

Certainly these are admirable, if expected, reasons to read Anne Bradstreet. We must ask, however, what she can truly say to us in light of our vastly different cultural, societal, and religious contexts. Herein lies an irony—perhaps what makes her different from us is exactly what makes a reading of her work so integral. Perhaps it is exactly our contextual differences and the effects they have on our perceptions of life and the afterlife that should propel us to read her work. Whether we recognize it or not, this voice resounding from another era faced the same ultimate realities we face today—the realities of a God-centered universe.

Bradstreet's culture, her surroundings, and her tradition, coupled with her spiritual and intellectual mettle, brought many of these pivotal truths to the forefront, truths that we tend to overlook on a daily basis. A colonist who was regularly confronted with impending death and the afterlife, she was constantly reminded of her mortality, for example, and lived in light of it. Our mortality may be masked by the niceties of modern living and medical advances, but it is still there, lurking beneath a seemingly solid but thin veneer and relentless in its ultimate grip. In contrast to the common delusion that we control our lives in today's society, we can gain in Bradstreet the perspective of one who recognized God's sovereign hand in every aspect of her life, in times of exuberance and in times of pain. And, through reading Bradstreet we can share the vision of a woman who possessed a sharp awareness of the holistic ways in which the doctrines of grace can and should permeate day-to-day living.

In spite of our seeming contextual differences, perhaps Bradstreet's perspective can remind us of what we *do* have in common. Why wouldn't we want to read Anne Bradstreet, or anyone else for that matter, who reminds us that in spite of our twenty-first-century context, we face the same realities of life—of mortality, of redemption, and of the role of grace? Perhaps Bradstreet's probing and self-reflection in light of these, a characteristically Puritan discipline, will inspire us toward the same, whether through literature or otherwise.

In order to assist the reader in exploring the work of this remarkable writer, this volume offers introductory chapters providing an overview of Bradstreet's life, spiritual and literary contexts, and critical reception. These chapters include a synopsis of Bradstreet's Puritan and British Renaissance roots, a discussion of the recurring themes and devices that emerge in her poems and prose, and a brief look at her reception among critics. A reader of poetry and prose follows, offering brief introductions to larger groupings of Bradstreet's work, as well as to individual poems and prose pieces, and providing footnotes to explain allusions and archaic words.

Most collections of Bradstreet present her works in chronological order. This volume groups the poetry strictly thematically with the hope that each section will reveal a different aspect of this multi-faceted woman. John Harvard Ellis's 1867 edition of Bradstreet's work (reprinted in 1932 and 1962) serves as the source for the poetry and prose. Ellis's edition, which was the first to print the contents of the Andover Manuscript book, contains what is essentially an edited reprint of the second edition of Bradstreet's poetry published by John Foster in 1678 in Boston. Most scholars consider the 1678 edition to better reflect Bradstreet's intentions than the 1650 first edition published without her knowledge. Although the typography and use of apostrophes presented in Ellis's edition have been updated, this volume otherwise follows the original punctuation, capitalization, and spelling of Ellis.

It is my hope that this volume will provide windows to the soul of Bradstreet. She merits the attention not only because she is such an intriguing historical figure and skilled poet, but also because she reminds us of the aesthetic and spiritual stimulation even centuries-old literature can provide to those willing to take the time to plumb it.

PART 1

BRADSTREET AND HER WORK

1

PILGRIM POET: THE LIFE OF ANNE BRADSTREET

Just three years before her death, Anne Bradstreet penned verses whose tired couplets describe a longing for eternity and escape from the cares of this world. Comparing herself to a "weary pilgrim" who has experienced such hardships as "burning sun," "stormy raines," "bryars and thornes," "hungry wolves," and "rugged stones," she voices her desire to complete her spiritually and physically taxing pilgrimage:

> A pilgrim I, on earth, perplext
>   with sinns with cares and sorrows vext
> By age and paines brought to decay
>   and my Clay house mouldring away

She longs for the resurrection and eternity spent with Christ, for release from her physical limitations and sufferings, and for freedom from separation and loss:

> Oh how I long to be at rest
>   and soare on high among the blest.
> This body shall in silence sleep

Mine eyes no more shall ever weep
No fainting fits shall me assaile
nor grinding paines my body fraile
With cares and fears ne'r cumbred be
Nor losses know, nor sorrowes see

No doubt, Bradstreet had good reason to be weary. She had survived the ravages of smallpox and had throughout her life endured numerous illnesses. She had experienced

KING JAMES I.

1.1 Portrait and autograph of James I, whose reign began nine years before Bradstreet's birth.

Old England at a time of brewing hostility toward the non-conformist Puritans under James I, Charles I, and the infamous Archbishop Laud. She had survived a potentially treacherous voyage to the New World and had borne up under the same harsh conditions in the Massachusetts Bay Colony that had snuffed out the lives of many of her fellow settlers. She had possessed for decades a firsthand view of the political and religious turmoil of a young colony experiencing growing pains that often embroiled her husband and father in conflict. And, later in life, she had experienced her own personal tragedies, including the burning of her house and the deaths of numerous family members.

Of course, this is not to mention that during these many hardships, Bradstreet had reared eight children. And she had negotiated the precarious role of a woman writer, becoming the first published American poet. To be sure, Bradstreet had lived an eventful life—certainly privileged in many ways, but likewise full of testing—and for this, she had good reason to relish eternal rest.

Life in Old England

Fifty-seven years earlier in 1612, she had been born Anne Dudley to Dorothy and Thomas Dudley in Northampton, England. Since no baptismal record survives, she documents for us her approximate birth date in a 1632 poem in which she describes herself as "Twice ten years old."

We know relatively little of Bradstreet's mother, Dorothy Dudley. Cotton Mather describes her in his *Magnalia Christi Americana* as "a Gentlewoman whose Extract and Estate were Considerable." Bradstreet herself extols her mother's numerous virtues, calling her a "Worthy Matron of unspotted life," "loving Mother and obedient wife," and "true Instructer of her Family." Apparently a woman who demanded much of others and gave liberally in exchange, she pitied and gave to the poor and was "To servants wisely aweful, but yet kind."

Bradstreet's father, Thomas Dudley, never attended university, though he apparently received a rigorous education at a free school in Northampton. Consistently recognized for his intellectual mettle and devotion to reading, he is described as a "devourer of books" by Cotton Mather and as a "Magazine of History" by Anne.

Orphaned at the age of ten after his father fell in battle as a soldier for Queen Elizabeth, the young Dudley grew to attain numerous positions of stature even in his youth. He served first as a page, then as a law clerk to Judge Nicolls in Northamptonshire, next as a captain under Queen Elizabeth in a war supporting the Protestant King Henry IV of France against Spanish forces, and again as a clerk for Nicolls, where Anne would have spent her first years.

Dudley rose to even greater prominence in 1619 when he was summoned to serve as steward of the affairs of Theophilus, Earl of Lincoln. The young earl, having recently inherited a debt-ridden estate from his father, looked to Dudley to bring order and prosperity to his affairs. This is just what Dudley did, and he was to continue in the earl's service until 1630, with a break of just a few short months.

Sitting Loose from God

Just seven when her father brought his young family to the earl's estate, which was comprised of Tattershall Castle and Sempringham Manor in County Lincolnshire, Anne found herself catapulted into a culturally and intellectually stimulating atmosphere. Living in the latter stages of the British Renaissance and the flowering of culture begun under Queen Elizabeth, she had an array of literature available to her in the earl's vast library. In addition to reading the Geneva Bible and metrical versions of the Psalms, she likely tasted the work of numerous classical poets, including Homer, Aristotle, Virgil, and Plutarch. She certainly imbibed the work of more recent writers, including Sir Walter Raleigh's *History of the World*, Joshua Sylvester's translation of Du Bartas's *Divine Weekes and Workes*, and Sir Philip Sidney's *Arcadia* and *Astrophel and Stella*, all of which heavily influenced her own poetic endeavors.

She also read in her youth and later in life the work of numerous other writers of the time and surely must have been at least familiar with the general tenor and content of Shakespeare's sonnets and plays, in spite of his ambivalent and often hostile reception among the Puritans. Living in the midst of a scientific and cultural revolution, she read numerous science and history writers whose influences later appear in her writings, as well.

By virtue of her gender, Anne did not join her older brother, Samuel, in outside schooling, yet she demonstrated her proclivity for learning and experienced an equally rich education at home. In addition to likely instruction from her father in foreign languages, perhaps including Greek, Latin, Hebrew, and French, she may have been tutored by Thomas Lodge, a poet and physician who was charged with educating the earl's own children.

In addition, Anne found herself in a hotbed of nonconformist thought while living in the earl's household. Theophilus often entertained the famed John Cotton, vicar of St. Botolph's Church in Boston, Lincolnshire, who was later to join the settlers in the New World. The earl's chapel in particular became a place where Puritans often preached and nonconformists met to exchange ideas and discourse upon the religious and political issues of the day.

All the while, Anne was taking note of her own soul's condition. In a letter titled "To my Dear Children," she records, "In my young years, about 6 or 7 as I take it, I began to make conscience of my wayes, and what I knew was sinfull, as lying, disobedience to parents, &c. I avoided it." She records her conscience being pricked when she did succumb to "like evills," drawing her to confession through prayer and the reading of scriptures. In typical Puritan fashion, she often connects the Lord's working and even correction in her

J Cotton

JOHN COTTON

1.2 Portrait and autograph of John Cotton, vicar of St. Botolph's Church in Boston, Lincolnshire, England, who later emigrated to the Massachusetts Bay Colony.

life to her physical afflictions. Experiencing a childhood ill-ness likely to have been rheumatic fever, she describes the situation as drawing her closer to God.

Such physical suffering was to be a rod of correction in Bradstreet's teenage years. She records that at fourteen or fifteen, her heart was "more carnall," and she was "sitting loose from God," controlled by "vanity and the follyes of youth." She proceeds to recount how the Lord chastened her for her spiritual wanderings: "About 16, the Lord layd his hand sore upon me and smott mee with the small pox." She adds, "When I was in my affliction, I besought the Lord and confessed my Pride and Vanity and he was entreated of me, and again restored me." Of course, this disease, which left its physical manifestations on the survivor, may have been a key element in deflating the pride she had described.

Any physical remnants of the disease did not seem to dis-suade Simon Bradstreet, however, who was destined to make Anne his wife during this same year. Anne was sixteen and Simon twenty-five. Simon was in many ways a mirror image of Anne's father. Orphaned at the age of fourteen, he came under the care of the Earl of Lincoln. Like Anne's older brother, Simon attended Emmanuel College of Cam-bridge, taking both bachelor's and master's degrees and then returning to serve as Dudley's assistant in running the earl's estate. Before and after their marriage, Simon also served as steward to the Countess of Warwick. Anne would later testify to the strength and true love of her union with Si-mon, writing, "If ever two were one, then surely we. / If ever man were lov'd by wife, then thee."

Marriage at sixteen, however, was young for someone of Anne's social station even by seventeenth-century standards, and some have suggested that this hastened marriage points to the growing religious and political tensions in England that compelled the Bradstreets and the Dudleys to consider emigration to the New World. These pressures had been simmering for years and were beginning to come to a head. At the 1604 Hampton Court Conference, King James, while decreeing a new English translation of the Bible, also declared his refusal to tolerate any nonconformity to the Church of England. He proclaimed, "I shall make them conform themselves or I will harry them out of the land."

CHARLES I.

1.3 Portrait and autograph of Charles I, whose quarrels with Parliament and persecution of nonconformists through Archbishop Laud led to the emigration of many Puritans and to civil war in 1642.

Later, his son Charles I had increased hostility toward non-conformists, particularly with his appointment of the infamous Archbishop Laud, whose zeal led to the persecution of those who preached dissident views.

Such political tensions were further incited by the material extravagance of the monarchy, as evidenced in the reigns of both James I and Charles I. Charles, who inherited the throne in 1625, particularly fanned the flames by demanding forced loans from his nobles in 1626 in order to support his court. When he joined other nobles in refusing such loans, the Earl of Lincoln was imprisoned in the Tower of London, a situation which could have resulted in beheading, as it often had for previous inhabitants of this infamous prison. Upset at his inability to control his nobles, Charles enraged them by suspending Parliament in 1629.

Visions of a New World

Such political and religious forces converged to speed the departure of the Dudleys and the Bradstreets to the New World. In 1629 both Thomas Dudley and Simon Bradstreet joined others in signing a patent to remove to America, and on March 20, 1630, Anne and her husband, as well as her parents and their family, boarded the *Arbella* for the voyage to the New World. The 350-ton ship, named after the Earl of Lincoln's sister, served as a flagship for three other ships, the *Talbot*, the *Ambrose*, and the *Jewell*.

The voyage itself, as documented in John Winthrop's journal, presented a number of perils. It was slow going at first, with stormy weather and contrary winds preventing the ships from leaving England until April 8. Once the journey was finally underway, the seafarers were soon roused to alarm by the appearance of eight ships of unknown and potentially enemy origin. Thinking they might be Dunkirk pri-

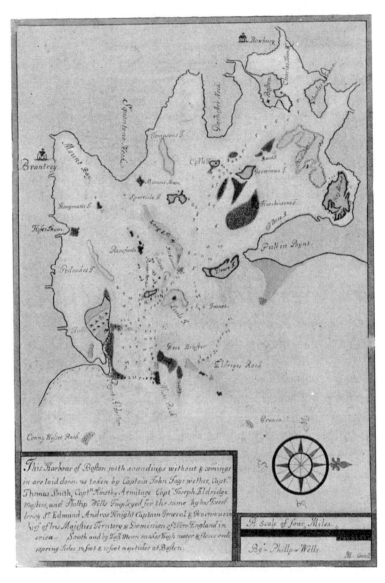

1.4 Early map of Boston Harbor, where Bradstreet first arrived in the New World.

vateers working for the government of Spain, the voyagers prepared for combat. Women and children were quickly corralled below the deck for safety, items liable to catch fire, such as bed mats, were thrown out of the ship, and firearms were poised for battle. Only upon nearing the ships did the travelers on the *Arbella* discover them to be peaceful, and, Winthrop notes, they praised God as "fear and danger [were] turned into mirth and friendly entertainment."

Of course, time and the elements provided enough challenge for the voyage. Many experienced seasickness in stormy seas, and as time went on, scurvy became a problem. At least two women gave birth on the ship, with the second giving birth to a stillborn baby. Close quarters also led to difficulties, with more than one passenger being placed in the stocks for inappropriate behavior, although Winthrop notes that this was much the exception.

On the way, the Massachusetts Bay Colony took its form, and Bradstreet surely would have heard Winthrop's "A Model of Christian Charity," purportedly written either just before or during the voyage to the New World. In this ad-

1.5 The arrival of the *Arbella* and company in Boston Harbor.

dress, Winthrop set out his famed vision of a "City upon a Hill," in which all settlers would work together in their respective stations to create a successful society. He also warned, however, that if the settlers were seduced by "other Gods," including "pleasures, and profits," they would "surely perish out of the good land."

1.6 Portrait and autograph of John Winthrop, who served as first governor of the Massachusetts Bay Colony and crafted the famed vision of a "City upon a Hill" in his "Model of Christian Charity" sermon.

On June 8, the travelers caught their first glimpse of this "good land," spotting two land birds and, according to Winthrop, experiencing "so pleasant a sweet ether as did much refresh" and detecting "a smell off the shore like the smell of a garden." Four days later, the ship pulled into the harbor at Salem.

A Howling Wilderness

First impressions for Anne and for most of the passengers, however, did not remain quite so idyllic as they encountered the ailing settlement of Salem and the heat of a New England summer. Not yet eighteen upon landing in the New World, Anne saw before her a world very different from the refinement and intellectual splendor of the earl's estate. She records her initial rebellion: "I found a new world and new manners, at which my heart rose." Although she notes that she later "was convinced it was the way of God, . . . and submitted to it and joined to the church at Boston," she is clear about her initial recoil from her new circumstances.

Indeed, to us, early New England may seem quaint and charming, but to the first-generation Puritans it was a howling wilderness. This wilderness, not for the fainthearted, took its toll upon the settlers. In the first few months, many died, including Lady Arbella and her husband. Winthrop himself experienced tragedy soon after landing when his son drowned while trying to retrieve a canoe. And many more were to face disease and near-starvation during the first harsh winter. In a letter to Lady Arbella's mother, Thomas Dudley compared the situation to the "Egiptians that there is not an house where there is not one dead, and in some houses many."

Surviving their first winter in Charlestown, the Bradstreets traveled up the Charles River to Cambridge. This was to be the first of numerous moves, each taking them to the edge of the wilderness. It was here that Bradstreet wrote her first extant poem, "Upon a Fit of Sickness, Anno. 1632," a poem in which she records once again coming near to death due to illness.

In addition to experiencing physical suffering in the New World, Bradstreet despaired at being childless. She records in her letter to her children, "It pleased God to keep me a long time without a child, which was a great greif to me, and cost mee many prayers and tears before I obtain one, and after him gave mee many more." In 1633, she gave birth to her first child, Samuel.

Of course, childbirth, though greatly desired by Anne, also brought imminent danger in a society with a staggering infant and maternal mortality rate. Acutely cognizant of this danger, she confesses her fear of death in childbirth and its resulting separation from her husband and children. In a poem written shortly before the birth of one of her children, she implores Simon to remember her and to protect her children from "step Dames injury."

Trouble in Paradise

Several years after their move to Cambridge, the Bradstreets once again uprooted themselves, along with Anne's parents and family, to move north to Ipswich. It was here that Anne was especially prolific in spinning out poetry, particularly her formal epics. It was also here that her husband's management skills and sizable land allowed him to prosper, becoming, as Cotton Mather describes him, a "venerable Mordecai of his country" and sometimes, as would be the case throughout his life, drawing the criticism of fellow Puritans, presumably jealous of his material wealth.

1.7 Initial word of the Massachusetts Bay Colony charter.

As had been the case in the Old World, religious and political tensions had been bubbling since the inception of the migration, and they often reared their heads in this new colony, as well. True to Winthrop's warning about the importance of unity in the colony, dispersion and a desire for land had become in recent years a source of contention. Winthrop himself became an object of controversy when free men realized that he had not been allowing them all the privileges and rights in government guaranteed by the colony's charter. As a result, the colonists did not re-elect Winthrop as governor, and Anne's father, who had been deputy governor and had experienced his own set of tensions with Winthrop, served as governor from 1634–35. Winthrop would, however, go on to attain the position again.

Further stresses resulted from the colony's precarious relationship with the English monarchy in the 1630s. Charles I, cognizant of the independent ways of the Massachusetts Bay Colony, announced that he was proceeding to terminate the colony's charter and that he would rule Massachusetts through a royal governor. Although he chose Ferdinando Gorges to serve in this capacity, growing turmoil in England guaranteed that this never happened. Gorges would have to be content instead with territory in Maine.

In addition to overtly political tensions, the young colony experienced numerous religious controversies. Roger Williams, for example, was banished for advocating separa-

1.8 Rendering of Anne Hutchinson preaching to a crowd in her house.

tion of church and state and went on to found Rhode Island. Causing far more trepidation in the young Massachusetts Bay Colony, however, was the Antinomian Controversy, which threatened to tear the colony apart and resulted in the banishment of Anne Hutchinson and numerous followers. Hutchinson, who had been a follower of John Cotton and was actually defended by him at least early in the controversy, took Cotton's covenant of grace doctrine much further by denying the role of good works as a sign of justification. Regularly preaching in her home, she maintained that she received direct revelation from God and thus threatened the established church.

Hutchinson faced two trials, the first in 1637 before the General Court and the second, a church trial, in the following year. In the first trial, Bradstreet's father and husband had firsthand seats to the proceedings due to their roles in civil government. Following the second trial, Hutchinson was banished from the colony. So great was the upheaval during the whole affair that many of her followers, dubbed "Hutchinsonians," were disarmed by order of Governor Winthrop in order to prevent potential civil war. Following her dismissal, Hutchinson felt the brunt of a community raw from controversy and emboldened against her. Her later miscarriage was widely publicized as having produced a devilish creature, and when Hutchinson was murdered by Indians in New York, many believed it to be the work of God.

Of course, true of most colonists' situations, conflict with the Native Americans had also been a constant source of anxiety. This peaked in 1637, when a dispute between the Puritans and the Pequots erupted in a full-blown war ending in Mystic, Connecticut, with the extermination of almost all of the Pequots. No doubt, life was not idyllic in the new colony. Yet, as Bradstreet expresses in her 1642 "A Dialogue between Old *England* and New," things were comparatively better in the New World, with tensions mounting in the old soon to result in England's own civil war.

In 1643, Anne experienced the death of her mother. And, in 1645, the Bradstreets made a final move to Andover, another frontier town. The Bradstreet quiver was by this time full with five children and another born just months after the move. By 1652, they were to complete their family of eight children. Once again, the Bradstreets prospered, this time with a twenty-acre property, with Simon owning a large sawmill and farm. One historian records that in 1650, the Bradstreet house was the "showplace of all the countryside."

Anne's father, however, did not join the family in Andover. Some suggest family division over appropriate responses to the Antinomian Controversy, with Anne herself writing in her epitaph for him, "Truths friend thou wert, to errors still a foe, / Which caus'd Apostates to maligne so." Others point to his remarriage less than four months after Anne's mother's death as a source of possible contention. In any case, the Bradstreets were joined by Anne's sister Mercy Dudley Woodbridge and her husband, John Woodbridge, who served as minister in the frontier community while Simon served as magistrate.

Her Hand a Quill Fits

It was this brother-in-law who took to London a manuscript of Bradstreet's poetry, purportedly without her knowledge or permission. In 1650 Stephen Bowtell published her manuscript under the title *The Tenth Muse Lately sprung up in America. Or Severall Poems, compiled with great variety of Wit and Learning, full of delight . . . By a Gentlewoman in those parts.* The volume sold for sixpence and met immediate success.

In a prefatory poem directed to Bradstreet herself, Woodbridge uses the metaphor of childbirth to describe what he knows will be Bradstreet's reaction to being exposed to the world's perusal: "I know your modest mind, / How you will blush, complain, 'tis too unkind: / To force a womans birth, provoke her pain, / Expose her labours to the Worlds disdain." No doubt, Woodbridge must have realized Bradstreet's own precarious position as a woman writer. John Winthrop expressed typical sentiments of the time when he wrote of fellow settler Anne Hopkins that she had gradually lost her "understanding and reason" through the reading and writing of many books. Winthrop explained that "if she had attended her household affairs and such things as belong to women, and not gone out of her way and calling to meddle in such things as are proper for men, whose minds are stronger, etc., she had kept her wits and might have improved them usefully and honorably in the place God had set her."

In contrast, Bradstreet is presented by Woodbridge in other prefatory remarks as a woman who has not neglected her family for her writing and who is eminently commendable in all her traits. The book is touted in several introductory verses by writers who also draw attention to Bradstreet's gender, commending her greatly, though occasionally doing so by distinguishing her from the rest of her sex.

Upon discovering the publication of her poetry, Bradstreet herself expressed a degree of ambivalence. She, too, was surely cognizant of the difficulty of being a woman writer in a man's world, although she was several times throughout her life to champion women's intellectual abilities. In her poem about Queen Elizabeth, she proclaims that Elizabeth "hath wip'd off th' aspersion of her Sex" and asserts, "Let such as say our Sex is void of Reason, / Know tis

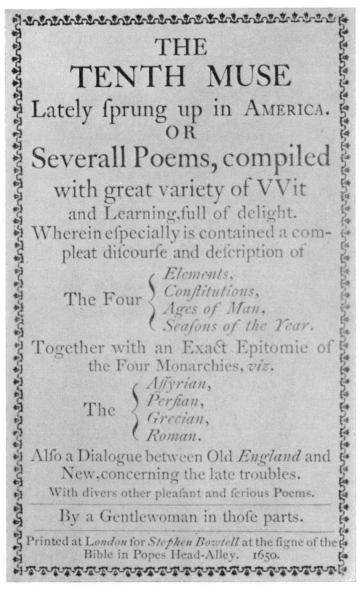

THE
TENTH MUSE
Lately fprung up in AMERICA.
OR
Severall Poems, compiled
with great variety of VVit
and Learning, full of delight.
Wherein efpecially is contained a compleat difcourfe and defcription of

The Four
- *Elements,*
- *Conftitutions,*
- *Ages of Man,*
- *Seafons of the Year.*

Together with an Exact Epitomie of
the Four Monarchies, *viz.*

The
- *Affyrian,*
- *Perfian,*
- *Grecian,*
- *Roman.*

Alfo a Dialogue between Old *England* and
New, concerning the late troubles.

With divers other pleafant and ferious Poems.

By a Gentlewoman in thofe parts.

Printed at *London* for *Stephen Bowtell* at the figne of the
Bible in Popes Head-Alley. 1650.

1.9 Title page of *The Tenth Muse*, the first edition of Bradstreet's work, published in London in 1650 from a manuscript carried there by her brother-in-law, apparently without her knowledge.

a Slander now, but once was Treason." In "The Prologue" to her poems, she also candidly admits, "I am obnoxious to each carping tongue / Who says my hand a needle better fits," yet she nonetheless asks for "some small acknowledgement" of the talents of women.

Much more disturbing to her than potential backlash due to her gender, however, was her embarrassment at the status of the published book. In "The Author to her Book," Bradstreet uses childrearing metaphors to confess her distress at seeing numerous errors caused by the printer. Describing her poetry as the "ill-form'd offspring of [her] feeble brain," she notes that "friends, less wise then true," took her work abroad and caused the unprepared manuscript "in raggs" to be published. In memorable lines she pens her reaction to the situation:

> At thy return my blushing was not small,
> My rambling brat (in print) should mother call,
> I cast thee by as one unfit for light,
> Thy Visage was so irksome in my sight;

Bradstreet also confesses, however, her maternal affection for her "rambling brat" and relates her attempts to remedy the defects of her manuscript, though with what she describes as little success. In any case, Bradstreet was now a published poet, and her work met with great reception both in the Old World and the New, regardless of any errors within.

Following the publication of her first book of poetry, Bradstreet continued to write, although her later poems as a whole took on a decidedly more personal note than the majority of her earlier epic work. Many of these later poems were inspired by events in her life, including her husband's and son Samuel's journeys to England. She recounts, for

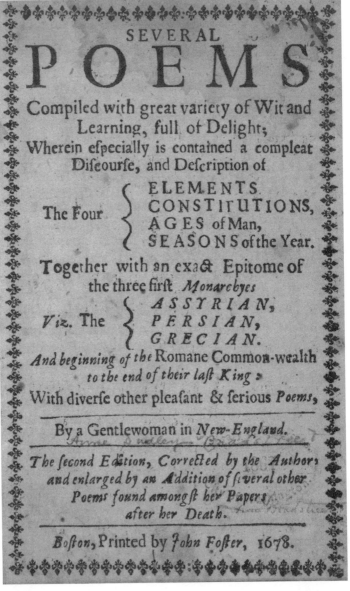

SEVERAL
POEMS

Compiled with great variety of Wit and
Learning, full of Delight;
Wherein especially is contained a compleat
Discourse, and Description of

The Four { ELEMENTS.
CONSTITUTIONS,
AGES of Man,
SEASONS of the Year.

Together with an exact Epitome of
the three first *Monarchyes*

Viz. The { *ASSYRIAN*,
PERSIAN,
GRECIAN.

And beginning of the Romane Common-wealth
to the end of their last King ;

With diverse other pleasant & serious *Poems*,

By a Gentlewoman in *New-England*.

*The second Edition, Corrected by the Author;
and enlarged by an Addition of several other
Poems found amongst her Papers
after her Death.*

Boston, Printed by *John Foster*, 1678.

1.10 Title page of *Several Poems*, the second edition of Bradstreet's work, published
posthumously in Boston in 1678, incorporating numerous revisions and eighteen new
poems.

example, her separation from her husband when he and John Norton were commissioned by the General Court to renegotiate the Massachusetts Bay charter with Charles II. The emissaries were successful in obtaining the charter, although they met with the disapproval of many in the colony, as they had agreed to religious toleration in exchange for the charter's renewal.

Bradstreet likewise testifies in numerous other poems to the power of illness and separation in her own life and in those around her, all the while pointing to the working of God through such suffering. She uses verse to help her process her emotions upon the deaths of several family members during this decade, particularly those of her son Samuel's four children and wife.

Tragedy of a different type visited the Bradstreet household on the night of July 10, 1666, as Anne was roused from her slumber by cries of "fire" which brought the Bradstreets' halcyon days of prosperity in their Andover home to an abrupt end. She records her emotion as she looked in the smoldering remains and remembered where particular belongings used to rest and where the family gathered for pleasant meals and tales. Although not mentioned in her poem, she also lost at least one manuscript she had been working on, and her son Simon records that his father's library of some eight hundred volumes was lost in the fire. Although she was to admit, "My pleasant things in ashes lye," she nonetheless ranked the experience with others for its role in molding her spiritual character. Indeed, in her sufferings, she followed her own advice to her children: "If at any time you are chastened of God, take it as thankfully and Joyfully as in greatest mercyes, for if yee bee his yee shall reap the greatest benefitt by it."

Of course, soon after, Bradstreet was also to pen "As Weary Pilgrim," and in 1672 she entered the heavenly rest for which she had longed, survived by her husband and seven of her eight children. As was customary, Simon remarried four years after Anne's death and went on to become deputy governor of the colony in 1678 and then governor in 1679–1686 and 1689–1692.

Six years after her death, Anne's work was to see a second edition. This time the book was published in Boston by John Foster, complete with her own corrections and with eighteen additional poems. It would see a third edition in 1758 and a first scholarly edition in 1867.

In early Puritan fashion, Bradstreet's burial plot boasted no gravestone or epitaph, and her unmarked grave is today unknown. There is a certain irony, however, that this Puritan woman, who gracefully defied convention of the day, firmly left her mark through language on the Massachusetts Bay Colony and on generations to come.

A Note on the Sources

Elizabeth Wade White provides the most comprehensive biography to date of Anne Bradstreet in *Anne Bradstreet: "The Tenth Muse"* (1971). Charlotte Gordon has recently offered another biography, *Mistress Bradstreet: The Untold Life of America's First Poet* (2005), in which she seeks not only to illuminate Bradstreet's life but also to explore her early American and Puritan contexts in general. Volumes containing biographical and critical introductions to Bradstreet's work include *The Works of Anne Bradstreet in Prose and Verse*, edited by John Harvard Ellis (1962), *The Works of Anne Bradstreet*, edited by Jeannine Hensley and with a foreword by Adrienne Rich (1967), *The Complete Works of Anne Bradstreet*, co-edited by Joseph R. McElrath Jr. and Allan P. Robb (1981), and *Early New England Meditative Poetry: Anne Bradstreet and Edward Tay-*

lor, edited by Charles E. Hambrick-Stowe (1988). Other volumes containing criticism and related biography include Josephine K. Piercy's *Anne Bradstreet* (1965), Wendy Martin's *An American Triptych: Anne Bradstreet, Emily Dickinson, Adrienne Rich* (1984), and Rosamond Rosenmeier's *Anne Bradstreet Revisited* (1991). *The Journal of John Winthrop, 1630–1649* is available in both full and abridged formats, edited by Richard S. Dunn and Laetitia Yeandle (1996). Cotton Mather's *Magnalia Christi Americana*, originally published in 1702, was edited by Kenneth B. Murdock (1977).

2

THE TENTH MUSE: READING ANNE BRADSTREET

When a collection of Anne Bradstreet's poetry first appeared without her knowledge in 1650, the book's title claimed that its anonymous writer was "The Tenth Muse, Lately sprung up in America." With such a designation, Bradstreet was purported to be following in the Greek tradition of the mythological Muses—the nine daughters of Zeus and Mnemosyne and the pagan goddesses of literature, dance, and music. While this characterization connects Bradstreet to the British Renaissance with its rediscovery of classical themes and mythology, other unsigned prefatory remarks in the volume, presumably by Bradstreet's brother-in-law John Woodbridge, draw attention to an equally, if not more important facet of this writer—her Puritan identity and vocation. Anticipating his readers' astonishment that a woman could have written the poetry, Woodbridge reveals, "It is the Work of a Woman, hounoured, and esteemed where she lives, for her gracious demeanour, her eminent parts, her pious conversation, her courteous disposition, her exact diligence in her place, and discreet managing of her Family occasions, and more then so, these Poems are the fruit but of some few houres, curtailed from her sleep and other refreshments." While his statement seeks to justify his sister-in-law's role as a woman poet in the seventeenth century, Woodbridge ultimately points to Bradstreet's overall piety and Puritanism.

Indeed, as these characterizations in the opening pages of *The Tenth Muse* reveal, the reader may find in Bradstreet, and in other Puritan writers of the time, two distinct, though not mutually exclusive, strains. Bradstreet was first and foremost a Puritan, but she was also a product of the British Renaissance. While some of her work reflects more of one facet than the other, a number of her poems heartily reflect both. In order to understand her impulses to verse, we must explore not only her Puritan worldview and aesthetic, but also her literary context and influences. And we might also find illumination through a brief survey of the insights of other readers since.

The British Renaissance

Spanning roughly from the end of the fifteenth century through the beginning of the seventeenth under the reign of the Tudors, the British Renaissance commenced later than its Italian counterpart but engendered a similar flowering of learning and culture. World exploration, military conquest, and expanded trade under the long and secure reign of Elizabeth I spawned optimistic intellectual exploits in numerous disciplines. The period boasted great forays into science with the ambitious scientific and philosophical work of Sir Francis Bacon (1561–1626), which was later to prompt the founding of the Royal Society of London in 1660. And it overflowed with countless works of drama and epic poetry and prose, with writers rekindling interest in classical themes, mythology, and ancient history—in essence, expansively reaching back to reclaim the splendors of ancient culture. Shining literary lights of the era included William Shakespeare (1564–1616), Edmund Spenser (c.1552–99), and even John Milton (1608–74), who, though living also in the Commonwealth era, shared many Renaissance characteristics.

These swirling currents of learning and culture particularly surface in Bradstreet's early work, including her lengthy quaternions and *The Four Monarchies*, where she displays—and perhaps even flaunts—encyclopedic knowledge and poetic skill. Both works demonstrate the length and epic scope of numerous Renaissance works. And both consider subjects classical in nature, with the quaternions discoursing on the elements, the humors, the ages of man, and the seasons and *The Four Monarchies* chronicling the civilizations of Assyria, Persia, Greece, and Rome.

The influences of specific writers, translators, and historians of the British Renaissance are most easily seen in *The Four Monarchies*. Sources of inspiration or actual material for this epic poem include, among others, Sir Walter Raleigh's unfinished *History of the World* (1614), which was written while he was imprisoned in the Tower of London; Archbishop Usher's *Annals of the World* (Latin 1650, English 1658); and Thomas North's translation of Plutarch (1579). Most influential on Bradstreet was the Calvinist poet Guillaume Du Bartas, who, though French, was essentially absorbed

2.1 Portrait of Sir Walter Raleigh, whose *History of the World* (1614) heavily influenced Bradstreet.

into the English Renaissance through Joshua Sylvester's eminently popular 1605 translation of his epic work on the seven days of creation. Bradstreet herself drew attention to Du Bartas's influence on her, and her contemporaries recognized his stamp on her poetry, with the Reverend Nathaniel Ward describing her as a "right *Du Bartas* Girle" in a poem prefacing *The Tenth Muse.*

Bradstreet's poetic retelling of British history also reflected an increasingly nationalistic Renaissance impulse to chronicle both the literal and mythical history of Britain. Other works demonstrating this include William Camden's *Britannia* (1586) and *Annals of Queen Elizabeth* (1615, 1625); Edmund Spenser's thinly disguised poetic epic about England and Queen Elizabeth, *The Faerie Queene*, which was left unfinished at his death in 1599; and Shakespeare's numerous history plays. While she did not make it the focus of her work, Bradstreet joined this rush to chronicle British history. Her "A Dialogue between Old *England* and New," though recounting the recent religious failings of England, contains a running log of historical events and famous figures. Decidedly much more celebratory, her elegy "In Honour of that High and Mighty Princess Queen Elizabeth of Happy Memory" describes Elizabeth as a figure towering over British and even world history.

Bradstreet also reveals through her elegies that she had caught at least a touch of the spirit of the age—the Renaissance humanism which applauded human capability and breadth. She praises Du Bartas as a model Renaissance figure due to his versatility, and she lauds the merits of the noble warrior and poet Sir Philip Sidney, who, she asserts, pleased the ancient gods of both war and poetry in his varied pursuits. And, in her tribute to Queen Elizabeth, Bradstreet presents Elizabeth not simply as a capable woman, but as an eminently capable human.

The general ornamentation and formal features of Bradstreet's poetry likewise disclose her Renaissance tendencies. She often writes in iambic pentameter couplets, also known as heroic couplets, although she occasionally employs more elaborate meter and rhyme schemes, as in "Contemplations," for example, where she utilizes a variation of the rhyme royal format. And the spirited dialogue and lively personification in her quaternions and in several shorter works, such as "A Dialogue between Old *England* and New" and "The Flesh and the Spirit," are essentially a carryover from Medieval literature that was also prevalent in the Renaissance period. This feature is evidenced in the work of Bradstreet's contemporary John Milton, whose Satan is often described as the most engaging of any character in *Paradise Lost*.

In addition to embracing many of the practices of Renaissance writers, Bradstreet exhibits and even anticipates strains of other seventeenth- and eighteenth-century literary movements. Using extended metaphors and clever conceits in poems about her family, Bradstreet shares a trait of the Metaphysical poets, such as John Donne (1572–1631). And, with her "Contemplations," she prefigures the Romantics' adulation of nature, although, of course, she curbs her exaltation by recognizing nature's place in the creative order. As a whole, however, Bradstreet's early epic work, as well as certain aspects of her later work, reflects the glories of Renaissance literature.

The British Reformation

Roughly concurrent with the British cultural Renaissance, the British Reformation also served to shape Bradstreet's work. The Anglican Church was inaugurated with the Act of Supremacy in 1534 when Henry VIII, who was seeking to divorce Catherine of Aragon, the first of his six wives, officially broke with the Roman Catholic Church. The Church of England was later solidified under Henry's son, Edward, and then further still by his daughter Elizabeth I. In 1559 Parliament passed another Act of Supremacy, largely in response to the intervening reign of Mary, to dissolve any remaining ties with Rome and install Elizabeth as the head of the Church. Although this new church distinguished itself from Rome in many ways, it also spawned the proliferation of Separatist groups, such as the Puritans, who desired further reform.

In their desire to purify the Church of England, the Puritans stressed a number of distinctives. Often characterized as "People of the Book," they set forward the centrality and primacy of Scripture, as opposed to church dogma. Hand in hand with this came a rejection of high church worship and ceremonial vestments, with a setting forth of the priesthood of the believer and of Christ's sufficiency in intercession. And Puritan preachers delivered the plain style sermon, intent on clarity rather than the verbal ornamentation and ritual liturgy often associated with the Anglican Church.

In doctrinal issues, the Puritans sought greater adherence to Calvinism than that practiced in the Church of England. They held as tantamount the doctrine of original sin, as expressed in the opening words of *The New England Primer*, "In Adam's fall, we sinned all." They also emphasized the depravity of human nature, thus tempering the optimistic humanism of the English Renaissance, and stressed human frailty and the transience of life, as evidenced in the *Primer*'s lines, "As runs the Glass, Man's life doth pass" and "Time cuts down all, Both great and small."

Though not generally attuned to the humanistic impulses of the Renaissance, the Puritans recognized the value of both reading and writing—and not simply reading and writing for purely religious ends. Bradstreet's father, for example, tried his hand at epic writing, perhaps in recognition of the same broad conception of the cultural mandate and validity of pursuing literature about God's world that Bradstreet herself possessed. Other persons and even institutions shared this conviction, as well. New England's Harvard insisted that all students who passed through its halls study and write poetry. Apparently many colonial readers heeded this call, for Cotton Mather was to warn nearly a century after against "a Boundless and Sickly appetite, for the Reading of Poems, which now the Rickety Nation swarms withal."

As might be expected, the Puritans used writing to promote their political, religious, and educational initiatives. They employed it polemically to critique the Anglican Church and even the Catholic Church, as evident in Bradstreet's "A Dialogue between Old *England* and New," where she decries the Anglican Church for its persecution of separatists and emulation of Catholic practices. And the Puritans wrote in order to enhance and even standardize education and worship, as evident in the colonies with *The New England Primer* and the *Bay Psalm Book* respectively.

The Puritans also turned to poetry to elucidate particular Scripture passages and theological truths. Bradstreet paraphrases biblical texts and concepts, as evident in her "*Davids Lamentation for Saul and Jonathan*" and "The Flesh and the Spirit." And, in much of her work, she reflects both implicitly and explicitly the Calvinistic belief of God's grand scheme of redemption. She acknowledges God's sovereignty throughout history in *The Four Monarchies*, for example, as well as human depravity and need for redemption in her "Contemplations." She was joined in this drive to narrate poetically God's role in history by her Puritan contemporary Michael Wigglesworth, whose wildly popular *The Day*

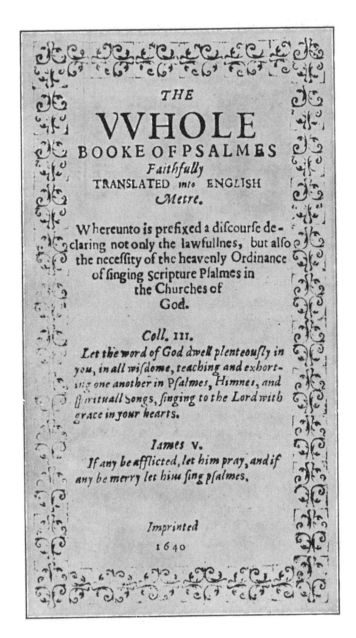

THE

VVHOLE

BOOKE OF PSALMES
Faithfully
TRANSLATED *into* ENGLISH
Metre.

Whereunto is prefixed a difcourfe declaring not only the lawfullnes, but alfo
the neceffity of the heavenly Ordinance
of finging Scripture Pfalmes in
the Churches of
God.

Coll. III.

*Let the word of God dwell plenteoufly in
you, in all wifdome, teaching and exhort-
ing one another in Pfalmes, Himnes, and
fpirituall Songs, finging to the Lord with
grace in your hearts.*

Iames V.

*If any be afflicted, let him pray, and if
any be merry let him fing pfalmes.*

Imprinted
1640

2.2 Title page of the *Bay Psalm Book*, used in the colony's worship services.

of Doom (1662) describes the concluding drama of history in the final judgment. Edward Taylor, the colonial minister and poet whose library contained only one volume of poetry—Bradstreet's—also took up the challenge of narrating God's work throughout the ages in his epic poem *Gods Determinations*, a work which was not published in his time but rediscovered by Thomas Johnson in 1936 in the Yale University Library. Though not a poet, Jonathan Edwards, often dubbed the "last Puritan," would a century after Bradstreet chronicle God's work throughout history in his ambitious sermon series *History of the Work of Redemption*, first delivered in Northampton, Massachusetts, in 1739 and published posthumously in 1774.

Perhaps the most popular use of writing and poetry among the Puritans, practiced with varying degrees of literary finesse, was a very personal one—that of facilitating meditation and introspection. This impulse in Bradstreet is best seen in her later and more personal lyrics and prose meditations. In these autobiographical pieces, unlike earlier works more reflective of her Renaissance tendencies, Bradstreet is synonymous with her speaker. Using her writing as a type of spiritual exercise or journal, she expresses the thoughts of her soul, confessing her foibles, giving voice to her desires, and declaring her aspirations for spiritual growth. Whereas her fellow Puritan John Milton wrote *Paradise Lost* in order to "justify the ways of God to man," Bradstreet wrote much of her personal work in order to reconcile *herself* to God and to work out the doctrines of her faith in everyday life.

Daniel Patterson has observed that Edward Taylor's poetic meditations became more of a process and less of a product as he matured. So, too, with Bradstreet, whose poems often demonstrate a distinct progression of thought, a record of her wrestling through spiritual issues. In many of

The DAY of
DOOM:

OR,

A Poetical Description

OF

The GREAT and LAST

Judgement.

WITH

A *Short* DISCOURSE about

Eternity.

By Michael Wigglesworth, Teacher of the
Church at *Maldon* in N. E.

The Fifth Edition, enlarged with
Scripture and *Marginal Notes.*

Acts 17. 31. *Because he hath appointed a day in the which he
will Judge the world in Righteousness, by that Man whom
He hath Ordained.* ------

Mat. 24. 30. *And then shall appear the Sign of the Son of
Man in heaven, and then shall all the Tribes of the earth
Mourn, and they shall see the Son of Man coming in the
clouds of heaven with power and great glory.*

BOSTON : Printed by B. *Green,* and *J. Allen,*
for *Benjamin Eliot,* at his Shop under the
West End of the Town-House. 1701.

2.3 Title page of fifth edition of Michael Wigglesworth's exceedingly popular *The Day of Doom* (1662), which both entranced and horrified readers with its descriptions of the last judgment.

her poems, Bradstreet displays a succession of reactions to her situation, responses which might be characterized as an earthly vision, a divine vision, and an eternal vision. For example, in her poem on the burning of her house, Bradstreet honestly admits her delight in earthly things and relationships, many of which are gifts from God, but which tend to take precedence in her life to the detriment of her focus on God. She acknowledges God's divine sovereignty in her earthly loss and concludes with an eye to eternity's unfading delights as both a corrective and a consolation. This pattern is clearly repeated in numerous other poems, but perhaps nowhere more poignantly than in her poetry about the deaths of her grandchildren and daughter-in-law.

Of course, Bradstreet often intended that her spiritual meditations might serve not only to reconcile herself to God but also to testify to her family about God's work in her life. In so doing, she, like the Puritan preachers of her day, sensed the urgency of her task and deliberately chose a plainer style than that characteristic of her early epic work. In some of her poetry about her sickness, for example, she mimics the familiar New England hymn meter. And, in her more spiritually focused poems as a whole, she seeks clarity rather than risk the potential obscurity of excessive ornamentation. Indeed, she hints at such an aim in the letter to her children prefacing her spiritual autobiography: "I have not studied in this you read to show my skill, but to declare the Truth—not to sett forth myself, but the Glory of God."

In her work at either end of the spectrum—whether the Renaissance inspired work of her early years or the more spiritually focused meditations of her later years—Bradstreet was fueled by a desire to glorify God. The scope of her oeuvre demonstrates that she possessed a broad vision of the ways in which literature might be used to glorify God, encompassing and unifying the aesthetic and the spiritual, the public and the personal. In following these impulses, impulses shaped by her age and by the spiritual redemption so central to her being, she produced literature both of its time and for all time.

Other Readers Along the Way

Of course, Bradstreet has met with varying degrees of admiration throughout the three-and-a-half centuries since she first broke into print. Even as her volume appeared in 1650, the critics were having their say, and most of it was overwhelmingly adulatory. Numerous commendatory poems and anagrams, signed only by initials but supplied by Bradstreet's friends and family, graced the introductory pages of the 1650 edition. Contributors of these poems who can be identified include, among others, Bradstreet's brother-in-law John Woodbridge; the Reverend Benjamin Woodbridge, brother of John; and Nathaniel Ward, Bradstreet's neighbor and minister at Ipswich and author of *The Simple Cobbler of Agawam* (1647).

These kind critics were lauding both Bradstreet herself and the contents of the 1650 volume, which boasted Bradstreet's dedication and prologue, quaternions and *The Four Monarchies*, "A Dialogue between Old *England* and New," elegies for Queen Elizabeth, Du Bartas, and Sir Philip Sidney, and biblical poems "*Davids Lamentation for Saul and Jonathan*" and "The Vanity of all worldly things"—all poems which were in step with traits a Renaissance reader would value. Indicative of their own debt to the Renaissance and in harmony with the volume's title, these critics employ a multitude of allusions to Greek and Roman mythology in their praises. Both John and Benjamin Woodbridge characterize Bradstreet as the tenth muse, and Nathaniel Ward presents a scenario in which Mercury and Minerva challenge Apollo to declare whether Du Bartas's or Bradstreet's work is superior.

Also reflective of the era, these praises are peppered with references to Bradstreet's gender. Bradstreet's critics just couldn't help themselves in expressing not simply their admiration for her achievements as a woman but also their astonishment that a woman *could* have written such accomplished work. Perhaps most conflicted in his praise is

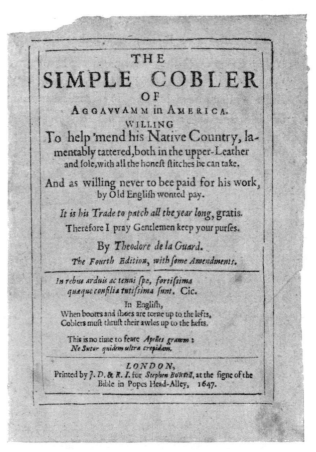

2.4 Title page of *The Simple Cobbler of Agawam* (1647), written by Nathaniel Ward, Bradstreet's neighbor and minister at Ipswich.

Nathaniel Ward, a writer who is well known among Bradstreet critics for having in his own book characterized certain women as having "squirrel brains." In addition to providing mitigated praise by portraying Bradstreet as an imitator of Du Bartas, he remarks, "It half revives my chil frost-bitten blood, / To see a Woman once, do ought that's good;" and then warns, "Let Men look to't, least Women wear the Spurrs."

John Woodbridge, who begins by deprecating his own poetic abilities in comparison to hers, also couches much of his praise in a dismissal of women's writing as a whole:

> If women, I with women may compare,
> Your works are solid, others weak as Air;
> Some Books of Women I have heard of late,
> Perused some, so witless, intricate,
> So void of sense, and truth, as if to erre
> Were only wisht (acting above their sphear)
> And all to get, what (silly Souls) they lack,
> Esteem to be the wisest of the pack.

While he admits that Bradstreet demonstrates great wit and ability and thus saves her gender from such an overriding stereotype, he presents her only as an exception: "That for a womans Work 'tis very rare." This type of a response to a woman poet—qualified adulation—surely explains Bradstreet's own comments in her prologue and her elegy for Elizabeth.

Nonetheless, both male and female readers found the 1650 edition extremely pleasing. A second edition, published posthumously in 1678 and including Bradstreet's numerous revisions as well as eighteen other poems, met with a similarly positive reception, and Bradstreet garnered praise for these two editions both in the colonies and in London. The first edition was featured with other well-known works in the bookseller London's catalog in 1658, and Milton's nephew Edward Phillips drew attention to it in his *Theatrum Poetarum* (1675). Early in the next century, Cotton Mather was also to praise Bradstreet's abilities, describing her work in his *Magnalia Christi Americana* (1702) as "a Monument for her Memory beyond the Statliest Marbles." Such appreciation of Bradstreet would largely wane, however, during the eighteenth and nineteenth centuries, with most of the critics perusing her work doing so condescendingly.

In spite of largely dismissive readings by critics during this period, several new editions did appear. A third edition, essentially a reprint of the second edition, was published in 1758. And, in 1867, John Harvard Ellis produced an especially noteworthy scholarly edition based on the 1678 *Several Poems* edition. In this volume, Ellis also published for the first time the contents of the Andover Manuscript Book, a leather-bound book containing several pieces in Bradstreet's own hand—her prose work "Meditations Divine and morall" and her poem "As Weary Pilgrim"—and several pieces copied into the book by her son Simon. While Ellis did readers a great service with this new edition, he joined his contemporaries at least partly in describing Bradstreet's poetry with terms such as "quaint and curious." And, in an 1897 edition of her poetry, Bradstreet's descendent Charles Eliot Norton similarly dismissed her poetry as only occasionally demonstrating excellence.

The twentieth century, however, brought with it a flowering of interest in and appreciation for Bradstreet, spurring even further editions. Most notable among these new editions are Josephine Piercy's 1965 facsimile reprint of the 1650 *The Tenth Muse* and the Andover Manuscript Book, Jeannine Hensley's edited and modernized 1967 publication of Bradstreet's work based on the 1678 *Several Poems* edition and the Andover Manuscript Book, Robert Hutchinson's 1969 thematically arranged edition of Bradstreet's poems based on the 1867 Ellis edition, Joseph R. McElrath Jr. and Allan P. Robb's 1981 meticulously annotated edition based primarily on the 1650 *The Tenth Muse*, and Charles Hambrick-Stowe's 1988 publication of Bradstreet's meditative poetry based on the 1867 Ellis edition in a volume also containing the poetry of Edward Taylor.

Commentary about Bradstreet's work and life has particularly flourished during the past half century, both in introductions to new editions and in other articles and full-length works. Just as the prefatory poems in the 1650 edition fixated on the person of Anne Bradstreet, as well as her gender, much of today's criticism is inseparable from speculation about Bradstreet herself. John Berryman, for example, drew critical acclaim with his provocative poem "Homage to Mistress Bradstreet," first published in 1953. And, many have looked to biography in order to illuminate Bradstreet's texts. Elizabeth Wade White, for example, in 1971 offered readers a comprehensive look into Bradstreet's life, as well as corresponding readings of her poems in tandem with biographical details. Others, such as Rosamond Rosenmeier, have attempted to parallel Bradstreet's writings with various phases of her life.

Of course, in their efforts to delve into the true identity of Bradstreet as a person and poet, the critics have focused on a number of different facets of her life and writing, resulting in varied and sometimes contradictory portraits. Most concentrate on Bradstreet's later lyrics and more personal writings, works which are comfortable and aesthetically pleasing to modern readers, although some critics have returned to probe the early epic work that so pleased Bradstreet's contemporaries. Feminist critics have been drawn to celebrate Bradstreet's abilities as a woman—particularly in practicing what was typically considered a masculine vocation—and to laud her outspoken comments on the abilities of women. Some critics have attempted to portray Bradstreet as the ultimately submissive Puritan, while others have advanced the picture of a creative rebel against Puritanism. Still others have closely examined her vision of spirituality. Charles Hambrick-Stowe, for example, has argued for parallels between Bradstreet and continental Catholic approaches to spirituality, as evidenced in Teresa of Avila (1515–1582). Indeed, the possible portraits of Bradstreet are as varied as the critics who examine her and her work.

In the end, perhaps it is best to understand the many facets of Anne Bradstreet through a number of these perspectives. She must be read as a colonial woman, quite comfortable in the cultural parameters set for her, yet challenging of the overarching stereotypes of her time which would preclude her from pursuing her literary craft and satisfying her intellectual curiosities. She must be read as one whose streams of literary influence included the British Renaissance, as one who appropriated the literary forms and styles of her time and even came to appreciate the spirit of her age, if tempered by her sense of the frailty and limitations of humanity. And, of course, she must be read as a Puritan, ultimately embracing a Puritan worldview and theology, yet honestly revealing in her work the process by which she wrestled with the sovereignty of God on the anvil of suffering and hardship. By reading Bradstreet biographically and contextually, we read her as she was in her own time. And by so doing, we also reap a richly contoured and seldom seen perspective.

A Note on the Sources

Elizabeth Wade White's *Anne Bradstreet: "The Tenth Muse"* (1971) and Rosamond Rosenmeier's *Anne Bradstreet Revisited* (1991) provide especially detailed close readings of much of Bradstreet's oeuvre, commenting on content, stylistic features, and biographical details affecting composition. Jeannine Hensley (1967), Joseph R. McElrath Jr. and Allan P. Robb (1981), and Charles E. Hambrick-Stowe (1988) offer criticism and summaries of Bradstreet criticism in their introductions to Bradstreet's work. Ivy Schweitzer's article "Anne Bradstreet Wrestles with the Renaissance" (1988) provides helpful insights on this topic. Daniel Patterson's edition of Edward Taylor's work (2003) offers a comprehensive introduction to Bradstreet's literary successor. John Berryman's poem is reprinted in numerous anthologies, but was originally published in book form in 1956. A number of other sources listed in the bibliography at the end of this book provide extensive commentary on Bradstreet's work and on her religious and literary contexts and influences.

PART 2

SELECTED WORKS OF
ANNE BRADSTREET

3

APPRENTICE

B radstreet regularly acknowledged her debt to the writers who had inspired and shaped her own work. And she just as regularly offered apologies for her own writing, as if in deference to these figures. While she felt compelled to deprecate her own abilities, partly due to the literary conventions of the day, she took issue with those who disregarded her work simply due to her gender.

As a younger poet, Bradstreet wrote five quaternions, epic poems of four parts each. The first four quaternions, titled "The Four Elements," "Of the Four Humours in Man's Constitution," "Of the Four Ages of Man," and "The Four Seasons of the Year," explore the diverse yet complementary natures of their subjects. Bradstreet's final and especially lengthy quaternion, "The Four Monarchies," chronicles the histories of Assyria, Persia, Greece, and Rome.

In 1642, Bradstreet presented the first two quaternions to her father, Thomas Dudley. Dudley had apparently written a similarly formatted work titled "On the four parts of the world." Although no extant copy of his poem exists, the piece may have been published, perhaps privately, for Bradstreet describes it as "cloth'd in black and white."

In her dedication, Bradstreet humbly acknowledges her inspiration by her father and the French poet Du Bartas. In her typical self-effacing fashion, she claims her inability to match their poetic skill and argues that her inferiority to Du Bartas demonstrates that she has not plagiarized his work. She references the personified speakers of her quaternions, who spar with one another for preeminence but ultimately work together in unity.

To her most Honoured Father *Thomas Dudley* Esq;
these humbly presented.

T. D. On the four parts of the world.

Dear Sir of late delighted with the sight
Of your four Sisters cloth'd in black and white,
Of fairer Dames the Sun, ne'r saw the face;
Though made a pedestal for *Adams* Race;
Their worth so shines in these rich lines you show   5
Their paralels to finde I scarcely know
To climbe their Climes, I have nor strength nor skill
To mount so high requires an Eagles quill;

Yet view thereof did cause my thoughts to soar;
My lowly pen might wait upon these four   10
I bring my four times four,[1] now meanly clad
To do their homage, unto yours, full glad:
Who for their Age, their worth and quality
Might seem of yours to claim precedency:
But by my humble hand, thus rudely pen'd   15
They are, your bounden handmaids to attend
These same are they, from whom we being have
These are of all, the Life, the Nurse, the Grave,
These are the hot, the cold, the moist, the dry,
That sink, that swim, that fill, that upwards fly,   20
Of these consists our bodies, Cloathes and Food,
The World, the useful, hurtful, and the good,
Sweet harmony they keep, yet jar oft times
Their discord doth appear, by these harsh rimes
Yours did contest for wealth, for Arts, for Age,   25
My first do shew their good, and then their rage.
My other foures do intermixed tell
Each others faults, and where themselves excell;
How hot and dry contend with moist and cold,
How Air and Earth no correspondence hold,   30
And yet in equal tempers, how they 'gree
How divers natures make one Unity
Something of all (though mean) I did intend
But fear'd you'ld judge *Du Bartas* was my friend
I honour him, but dare not wear his wealth   35
My goods are true (though poor) I love no stealth
But if I did I durst not send them you
Who must reward a Thief, but with his due.
I shall not need, mine innocence to clear
These ragged lines, will do't, when they appear: 40
On what they are, your mild aspect I crave
Accept my best, my worst vouchsafe a Grave.

---

1 **four times four**: "four; and four" in the 1650 edition to reflect the two
quaternions Bradstreet presented to Dudley in 1642

From her that to your self, more duty owes
Then water in the boundess Ocean flows.

March 20. 1642.

ANNE BRADSTREET.

This prologue introduces Bradstreet's quaternions, particularly "The Four Monarchies." Following in the self-deprecating spirit of her dedication, Bradstreet claims in stanzas one through four that she is neither a competent poet nor historian. She describes her jealousy of Du Bartas and her dismay that the muses seem to have given him an inordinate share of skill, leaving little for her. She also compares herself unfavorably to Demosthenes, the "sweet tongu'd Greek" who formerly "lisp'd" but overcame his speech deficiencies by trying to outshout the ocean.

Stanzas five through eight take a greatly different tone, moving from self-deprecation to self-assertion. Bradstreet notes that some find her "obnoxious" as a poet not because of the content of her poetry but because of her gender. Such critics claim that anything good she has written was "stoln" or "by chance." She submits tongue in cheek to the judgment that "[m]en can do best," while she simultaneously asks for some recognition of her talent—if not for the traditional bayes of the poet, at least for a more domestic wreath of thyme or parsley. Critics note her clever irony in describing these herbs as a consolation prize, for the Greeks attached connotations of honor and strength to them.

The Prologue.

1.

To sing of Wars, of Captains, and of Kings,
Of Cities founded, Common-wealths begun,
For my mean pen are too superiour things:
Or how they all, or each their dates have run
Let Poets and Historians set these forth,   5
My obscure Lines shall not so dim their worth.

2.

But when my wondring eyes and envious heart
Great *Bartas* sugar'd lines, do but read o're
Fool I do grudg the Muses did not part
'Twixt him and me that overfluent store;   10
A *Bartas* can, do what a *Bartas* will
But simple I according to my skill.

3.

From school-boyes tongue no rhet'rick we expect
Nor yet a sweet Consort from broken strings,
Nor perfect beauty, where's a main defect: 15
My foolish, broken, blemish'd Muse so sings
And this to mend, alas, no Art is able,
'Cause nature, made it so irreparable.

4.

Nor can I, like that fluent sweet tongu'd Greek,
Who lisp'd at first, in future times speak plain   20
By Art he gladly found what he did seek
A full requital of his, striving pain
Art can do much, but this maxime's most sure
A weak or wounded brain admits no cure.

5.

I am obnoxious to each carping tongue   25
Who says my hand a needle better fits,
A Poets pen all scorn I should thus wrong,
For such despite they cast on Female wits:
If what I do prove well, it won't advance,
They'l say it's stoln, or else it was by chance.   30

6.

But sure the Antique Greeks were far more mild
Else of our Sexe, why feigned they those Nine
And poesy made, *Calliope*'s own Child;[2]
So 'mongst the rest they placed the Arts Divine,
But this weak knot, they will full soon untie,   35
The Greeks did nought, but play the fools & lye.

7.

Let Greeks be Greeks, and women what they are
Men have precedency and still excell,
It is but vain unjustly to wage warre;
Men can do best, and women know it well   40
Preheminence in all and each is yours;
Yet grant some small acknowledgement of ours.

8.

And oh ye high flown quills that soar the Skies,
And ever with your prey still catch your praise,
If e're you daigne these lowly lines your eyes   45
Give Thyme or Parsley wreath, I ask no bayes,
This mean and unrefined ure of mine
Will make you glistring gold, but more to shine.

---

2 **Calliope's own Child:** in ancient Greek myth, the poet Orpheus, who
was said to be the child of Calliope, the muse of epic poetry

Bradstreet crafted a number of elegies. Here she praises the French Calvinist poet Guillaume Du Bartas (1544–1590), from whom she drew inspiration for her own work. Du Bartas's poetry had recently been translated into English by Joshua Sylvester and published as *Bartas: His Devine Weekes and Workes* (1605), a volume which met with instant success in England.

Bradstreet celebrates Du Bartas as possessing a wide range of knowledge and skill—a true Renaissance man—and as excelling in fame and abilities beyond other notable Frenchmen. Unfortunately, her predictions of his enduring fame have not materialized. As has been her characteristic approach, Bradstreet includes in her poem a healthy dose of self-deprecation, writing that her muse is infantile, a "silly pratler [who] speaks no word of sense."

In honour of *Du Bartas*, 1641.

> Among the happy wits this age hath shown,
> Great, dear, sweet *Bartas* thou art matchless known;
> My ravish'd Eyes and heart with faltering tongue,
> In humble wise have vow'd their service long,
> But knowing th' task so great, & strength but small,   5
> Gave o're the work before begun withal,
> My dazled sight of late review'd thy lines,
> Where Art, and more then Art, in nature shines,
> Reflection from their beaming Altitude,
> Did thaw my frozen hearts ingratitude;   10
> Which Rayes darting upon some richer ground,
> Had caused flours and fruits soon to abound;
> But barren I my Dasey here do bring,
> A homely flour in this my latter Spring,
> If Summer, or my Autumn age do yield,   15

Flours, fruits, in Garden, Orchard, or in Field,
They shall be consecrated in my Verse,
And prostrate offered at great *Bartas* Herse;
My muse unto a Child I may compare,
Who sees the riches of some famous Fair,   20
He feeds his Eyes, but understanding lacks
To comprehend the worth of all those knacks:
The glittering plate and Jewels he admires,
The Hats and Fans, the Plumes and Ladies tires,
And thousand times his mazed mind doth wish   25
Some part (at least) of that brave wealth was his,
But seeing empty wishes nought obtain,
At night turns to his Mothers cot again,
And tells her tales, (his full heart over glad)
Of all the glorious sights his Eyes have had: 30
But finds too soon his want of Eloquence,
The silly pratler speaks no word of sense;
But seeing utterance fail his great desires,
Sits down in silence, deeply he admires:
Thus weak brain'd I, reading thy lofty stile,   35
Thy profound learning, viewing other while;
Thy Art in natural Philosophy,
Thy Saint like mind in grave Divinity;
Thy piercing skill in high Astronomy,
And curious insight in Anatomy: 40
Thy Physick, musick and state policy,
Valour in war, in peace good husbandry.
Sure lib'ral Nature did with Art not small,
In all the arts make thee most liberal.
A thousand thousand times my sensless sences   45
Moveless stand charm'd by thy sweet influences;
More sensless then the stones to *Amphions* Lute,[3]
Mine eyes are sightless, and my tongue is mute,
My full astonish'd heart doth pant to break,
Through grief it wants a faculty to speak: 50

3 **Amphions Lute:** in Greek myth, Amphion's music, which was said to
move stones into place in the building of the wall around Thebes

Volleyes of praises could I eccho then,
Had I an Angels voice, or *Bartas* pen:
But wishes can't accomplish my desire,
Pardon if I adore, when I admire.
O France thou did'st in him more glory gain   55
Then in thy *Martel, Pipin, Charlemain*,[4]
Then in St. *Lewes*, or thy last *Henry* Great,[5]
Who tam'd his foes in warrs, in bloud and sweat.
Thy fame is spread as far, I dare be bold,
In all the Zones, the temp'rate, hot and cold.   60
Their Trophies were but heaps of wounded slain,
Thine, the quintessence of an heroick brain.
The oaken Garland ought to deck their brows,
Immortal Bayes to thee all men allows.
Who in thy tryumphs never won by wrongs,   65
Lead'st millions chaind by eyes, by ears, by tongues
Oft have I wondred at the hand of heaven,
In giving one what would have served seven.
If e're this golden gift was showr'd on any,
Thy double portion would have served many.   70
Unto each man his riches is assign'd
Of Name, of State, of Body and of Mind:
Thou hadst thy part of all, but of the last,
O pregnant brain, O comprehension vast:
Thy haughty Stile and rapted wit sublime   75
All ages wondring at, shall never climb.
Thy sacred works are not for imitation,
But Monuments to future Admiration.
Thus *Bartas* fame shall last while starrs do stand,
And whilst there's Air or Fire, or Sea or Land.   80
But least mine ignorance should do thee wrong,
To celebrate thy merits in my Song.
I'le leave thy praise to those shall do thee right,
Good will, not skill, did cause me bring my Mite.

4 **Martel, Pipin, Charlemain:** all Frankish rulers, with Charlemain also becoming the first Holy Roman Emperor
5 **St. Lewes, . . . last Henry Great:** King Louis IX of France and King Henry IV of France and Navarre

His Epitaph.

Here lyes the Pearle of *France*, *Parnassus*[6] Glory; 85

The World rejoyc'd at's birth, at's death was sorry.
Art and Nature joyn'd, by heavens high decree
Now shew'd what once they ought, Humanity:
And Natures Law, had it been revocable
To rescue him from death, Art had been able. 90
But Nature vanquish'd Art, so *Bartas* dy'd;
But Fame out-living both, he is reviv'd.

This short, witty verse is appended to the end of "The Four Seasons" quaternion. It displays Bradstreet's characteristic humility and desire to inform the reader that her poem contains flaws and that, in this case, her creativity seems to have waned during the writing process.

An Apology.

My Subjects bare, my Brain is bad,
Or better Lines you should have had:
The first fell in so nat'rally,
I knew not how to pass it by;
The last, though bad I could not mend, 5
Accept therefore of what is pen'd,
And all the faults that you shall spy
Shall at your feet for pardon cry.

6 **Parnassus:** mountain in Greece

Of all her epic poetry, "The Four Monarchies" presented Bradstreet with the greatest challenge, becoming her nemesis for several reasons. The 1650 edition of "The Four Monarchies" contains lines in which she admits the brevity of the section on Rome due to her "Shortnesse of time, and inability" resulting in "a confus'd brevity." In spite of her limitations, she contends, "Yet in this Chaos, one shall easily spy, / The vast limbs of a mighty Monarchy. / What e're is found amisse, take in best part. / As faults proceeding from my head, not heart."

After the publication of the 1650 edition, Bradstreet spent considerable effort to expand and edit this quaternion, particularly the final section on Rome. The following "apology," appended to the 1678 version of "The Four Monarchies," recounts her continued difficulty in completing the poem—a challenge much more dramatic than the time constraints that had previously vexed her, with her new manuscript destroyed by the fire that burned her Andover house to the ground in 1666. In spite of this loss, the second edition contains substantial changes and additions. Critics especially recognize the influence of Sir Thomas North's recent translation of Plutarch's *Lives* (1579) on the revised edition of "The Four Monarchies."

An Apology.

> To finish what's begun, was my intent,
> My thoughts and my endeavours thereto bent;
> Essays I many made but still gave out,
> The more I mus'd, the more I was in doubt:
> The subject large my mind and body weak,   5

With many moe discouragements did speak.
All thoughts of further progress laid aside,
Though oft perswaded, I as oft deny'd,
At length resolv'd, when many years had past,
To prosecute my story to the last;   10
And for the same, I hours not few did spend,
And weary lines (though lanke) I many pen'd:
But 'fore I could accomplish my desire,
My papers fell a prey to th' raging fire.
And thus my pains (with better things) I lost,   15
Which none had cause to wail, nor I to boast.
No more I'le do sith I have suffer'd wrack,
Although my Monarchies their legs do lack:
Nor matter is't this last, the world now sees,
Hath many Ages been upon his knees.   20

Bradstreet apparently had no knowledge that the Reverend John Woodbridge, her brother-in-law, took a number of her poems with him to London, resulting in the publication of the first edition of her poetry, *The Tenth Muse Lately Sprung Up in America* (1650). The following poem, included in the second edition (1678), describes Bradstreet's dismay at the first edition, with printing errors heightening what she considered the flaws of a manuscript not yet ready for the scrutiny of the outside world. She likens *The Tenth Muse* to a homely child, loved by mother yet distressing to her.

The Author to Her Book.

Thou ill-form'd offspring of my feeble brain,
Who after birth did'st by my side remain,
Till snatcht from thence by friends, less wise then true

Who thee abroad, expos'd to publick view,
Made thee in raggs, halting to th' press to trudg,   5
Where errors were not lessened (all may judg)
At thy return my blushing was not small,
My rambling brat (in print) should mother call,
I cast thee by as one unfit for light,
Thy Visage was so irksome in my sight;   10
Yet being mine own, at length affection would
Thy blemishes amend, if so I could:
I wash'd thy face, but more defects I saw,
And rubbing off a spot, still made a flaw.
I stretcht thy joynts to make thee even feet,   15
Yet still thou run'st more hobling then is meet;
In better dress to trim thee was my mind,
But nought save home-spun Cloth, i'th' house I find
In this array, 'mongst Vulgars mayst thou roam
In Criticks hands, beware thou dost not come;   20
And take thy way where yet thou art not known,
If for thy Father askt, say, thou hadst none:
And for thy Mother, she alas is poor,
Which caus'd her thus to send thee out of door.

Fig. 3.1 Anne Bradstreet and Her Times

c. 1612	Anne Dudley born in Northampton, England
1619–1630	Father, Thomas Dudley, serves as steward to Theophilus, Earl of Lincoln
1628	Suffers from smallpox; marries Simon Bradstreet
1630	Voyages to the New World aboard the *Arbella*; settles first in Salem, then Boston, then Cambridge
1632	Writes first dated poem
1633	Gives birth to her first child, Samuel
1634–1635	Father serves as governor of the Massachusetts Bay Colony
1635	Moves to Ipswich
1643	Mother, Dorothy Yorke Dudley, dies
1645	Moves to Andover, her final home
1650	*The Tenth Muse* is published, presumably without her knowledge
1652	Gives birth to last of her eight children
1653	Father dies
1662	Husband travels to England to renegotiate colony's charter
1665–1669	Several grandchildren and a daughter-in-law die
1666	House in Andover burns
1672	Dies September 16
1678	*Several Poems* is published posthumously
1679–1686	Husband serves as governor of the colony after her
1689–1692	death

1603	Elizabeth I dies (reigned 1558–1603); James I ascends to throne
1604	Hampton Court Conference convenes
1608	John Milton born (d. 1674)
1614	*History of the World* by Sir Walter Raleigh (c. 1552–1618) is published
1616	Shakespeare dies (b. 1564)
1625	James I dies; Charles I ascends to throne
1629	Charles I suspends Parliament
1631	John Donne dies (b. 1572)
1633	George Herbert dies (b. 1593)
1637	Pequot War erupts
1637, 1638	Civil and church trials of Anne Hutchinson occur
1642	English Civil War erupts
c. 1644	Edward Taylor born (d. 1729)
1647	Westminster Confession of Faith is written
1649	Trial and execution of Charles I occurs
1653	Oliver Cromwell (1599–1658) becomes Lord Protector
1660	Charles II is restored to throne
1662	*The Day of Doom* by Michael Wigglesworth (1631–1705) is published

4

BARD

Bradstreet is most appreciated by critics today for her more personal lyrics, although she composed a number of poems more epic in scope and typically classical, biblical, or political in subject. While her lengthy quaternions constitute the bulk of this poetry, the shorter poems reprinted here offer a taste of Bradstreet's more formal style.

This poem considers the religious and political conflict brewing in England, including quarrels between Charles I and Parliament and the persecution of dissenters under Archbishop Laud, which eventually ignited civil war in 1642. As a recent emigrant from England, Bradstreet viewed the tumult in her mother country with mixed emotions. Throughout the poem, personified New-England demonstrates true concern for her mother, albeit a desire that Old England's troubles will lead to her purification.

After New-England inquires about the cause of the current situation—whether it has been brought about by foreign foes, deposed monarchs, warring kingly lines, or plague, all of which have afflicted England in the past—Old England identifies the cause as general political and religious corruption, including the Catholicization of the Anglican Church and the persecution of dissenters. Old England admits that she should have learned from the examples of other countries, whose religious persecution led to judgment. New-England urges her mother to embrace a righteous political and religious structure, making recompense for previous faults. She even envisions a newly purified England vanquishing Catholic Rome and Islamic Turkey.

The 1678 version of the poem reprinted here takes into account the restoration of Charles II and thus differs slightly from the 1650 edition, which is more outspoken on the specific transgressions of the Anglican Church. Although supportive of the monarchy, the first edition is also more outrightly approving of Parliament, as evident in its second to last line, "Farewell dear mother, Parliament, prevail," which is changed to "Farewel dear Mother, rightest cause prevail" in the 1678 version. Bradstreet similarly altered the second edition of the "Old Age" section of her quaternions, calling Cromwell "an Usurper."

Here Bradstreet uses a dialogue format similar to that of her quaternions. The more serious nature of her topic in this poem, however, precludes the type of saucy banter common to her quaternions.

A Dialogue between Old *England* and New; concerning their present Troubles, *Anno*, 1642.

New-England.

Alas dear Mother, fairest Queen and best,
With honour, wealth, and peace, happy and blest;
What ails thee hang thy head, & cross thine arms?
And sit i'th' dust, to sigh these sad alarms?
What deluge of new woes thus over-whelme   5
The glories of thy ever famous Realme?
What means this wailing tone, this mournful guise?
Ah, tell thy daughter, she may sympathize.

Old England.

Art ignorant indeed of these my woes?
Or must my forced tongue these griefs disclose?   10
And must myself dissect my tatter'd state,
Which 'mazed Christendome stands wondring at?
And thou a Child, a Limbe, and dost not feel
My fainting weakned body now to reel?
This Physick purging potion, I have taken,   15
Will bring consumption, or an Ague[1] quaking,
Unless some Cordial, thou fetch from high,
Which present help may ease my malady.
If I decease, dost think thou shalt survive?
Or by my wasting state dost think to thrive?   20
Then weigh our case, if't be not justly sad;
Let me lament alone, while thou art glad.

---

1 **Ague:** fever and chills

New-England.

And thus (alas) your state you much deplore
In general terms, but will not say wherefore:
What medicine shall I seek to cure this woe,   25
If th' wound so dangerous I may not know.
But you perhaps, would have me ghess it out:
What hath some *Hengist*[2] like that *Saxon* stout
By fraud or force usurp'd thy flowring crown,
Or by tempestuous warrs thy fields trod down?   30
Or hath *Canutus*,[3] that brave valiant *Dane*
The Regal peacefull Scepter from thee tane?
Or is't a *Norman*,[4] whose victorious hand
With English blood bedews thy conquered land?
Or is't Intestine warrs that thus offend?   35
Do *Maud* and *Stephen*[5] for the crown contend?
Do Barons rise and side against their King,
And call in foraign aid to help the thing?
Must *Edward*[6] be depos'd? or is't the hour
That second *Richard*[7] must be clapt i'th tower?   40
Or is't the fatal jarre, again begun
That from the red white pricking roses[8] sprung?
Must *Richmonds* aid,[9] the Nobles now implore?

2 **Hengist:** 5th-century Saxon chieftain

3 **Canutus:** Canute the Great, 11th-century Danish King of England

4 **a Norman:** Duke William of Normandy, who became William I (William the Conqueror) after defeating Harold, Earl of Wessex at the Battle of Hastings in 1066

5 **Maud and Stephen:** Matilda, daughter of Henry I, and Stephen, grandson of William the Conqueror and nephew of Henry I, who warred against one another for the English throne in the 12th century, causing great anarchy

6 **Edward:** Edward II, who was forced from the throne and then murdered in 1327 when his estranged wife, Isabella, and Roger Mortimer conspired to put his son Edward III on the throne

7 **second Richard:** Richard II, who was imprisoned in Pontefract Castle, where he was murdered in 1400

8 **red white pricking roses:** the Wars of the Roses (1455–1485) between the House of Lancaster (red rose) and the House of York (white rose)

9 **Richmonds aid:** aid given by the Duke of Buckingham to exiled Lancastrian Henry Tudor, Earl of Richmond, who then became Henry VII by defeating Richard III in 1485

To come and break the Tushes of the Boar,[10]
If none of these dear Mother, what's your woe? 45
Pray do you fear *Spains* bragging *Armado*?[11]
Doth your Allye, fair *France*, conspire your wrack,
Or do the *Scots* play false, behind your back?
Doth *Holland* quit you ill for all your love?
Whence is the storm from Earth or Heaven above? 50
Is't drought, is't famine, or is't pestilence?
Dost feel the smart, or fear the Consequence?
Your humble Child intreats you, shew your grief,
Though Arms, nor Purse she hath for your relief,
Such is her poverty: yet shall be found 55
A Suppliant for your help, as she is bound.

Old England.

I must confess some of those sores you name,
My beauteous body at this present maime;
But forreign foe, nor feigned friend I fear,
For they have work enough (thou knowst) elsewhere 60
Nor is it *Alcies* Son, nor *Henryes* daughter;[12]
Whose proud contention cause this slaughter,
Nor Nobles siding, to make *John*[13] no King,
French *Lewis*[14] unjustly to the Crown to bring;
No *Edward*, *Richard*,[15] to lose rule and life, 65
Nor no *Lancastrians*[16] to renew old strife:

---

10 **Tushes of the Boar:** "tusks" of the Boar; reference to Richard III, as in Shakespeare
11 **Armado:** Spanish Armada, which was defeated by the English fleet under Queen Elizabeth in 1588
12 **Alcies Son, . . . Henryes daughter:** Stephen (son of Alice) and Matilda, mentioned earlier in the poem
13 **John:** King John, whose nobles rebelled, forcing him to sign the Magna Carta in 1215
14 **French Lewis:** Louis VIII of France, who was asked by English barons to invade England after John broke the terms of the Magna Carta
15 **Edward, Richard:** Edward II, Richard II, both mentioned earlier in the poem
16 **Lancastrians:** House of Lancaster

No Duke of *York*, nor Earl of *March*[17] to soyle
Their hands in kindreds blood whom they did foil
No crafty Tyrant now usurps the Seat,
Who Nephews slew[18] that so he might be great;   70
No need of *Tudor*,[19] Roses to unite,
None knows which is the red, or which the white;
Spains braving Fleet, a second time is sunk,
France knows how oft my fury she hath drunk:
By *Edward* third, and *Henry* fifth of fame,   75
Her Lillies in mine Arms avouch the same.
My Sister *Scotland* hurts me now no more,
Though she hath been injurious heretofore;
What *Holland* is I am in some suspence?
But trust not much unto his excellence.   80
For wants, sure some I feel, but more I fear,
And for the Pestilence, who knows how near;
Famine and Plague,[20] two Sisters of the Sword,
Destruction to a Land, doth soon afford:
They're for my punishment ordain'd on high,   85
Unless our tears prevent it speedily.
But yet I Answer not what you demand,
To shew the grievance of my troubled Land?
Before I tell th' Effect, I'le shew the Cause
Which are my sins the breach of sacred Laws,   90
Idolatry supplanter of a Nation,
With foolish Superstitious Adoration,
Are lik'd and countenanc'd by men of might,

---

17 **Duke of York, . . . Earl of March:** Edmund Plantagenet, who founded the House of York, and Roger Mortimer, Earl of March, mentioned earlier in the poem

18 **No crafty Tyrant . . . Who Nephews slew:** Richard III, who reputedly killed his own nephews, Edward and Richard, in the Tower of London in 1483; in the 1650 edition of the poem, Richard III is instead called a "Crook-backt-Tyrant"

19 **Tudor:** the Tudor dynasty, created by the uniting of the Houses of Lancaster and York with the marriage of Henry VII to Elizabeth of York in 1486, as represented in the Tudor rose, which contains a red center and white periphery

20 **Plague:** the Bubonic Plague

The Gospel troden down and hath no right:
Church Offices were sold and bought for gain,   95
That Pope had hope to find, *Rome* here again,
For Oaths and Blasphemies, did ever Ear,
From *Belzebub*[21] himself such language hear;
What scorning of the Saints of the most high?
What injuries did daily on them lye?   100
What false reports, what nick-names[22] did they take
Not for their own, but for their Masters sake?
And thou poor soul, wert jeer'd among the rest,
Thy flying for the truth was made a jest.
For Sabbath-breaking, and for drunkenness,   105
Did ever land profaness more express?
From crying blood yet cleansed am not I,
Martyres and others, dying causelesly.
How many princely heads on blocks laid down
For nought but title to a fading crown?   110
'Mongst all the crueltyes by great ones done
Of *Edwards* youth,[23] and *Clarence* hapless son,[24]
O *Jane*[25] why didst thou dye in flowring prime?
Because of royal stem, that was thy crime.
For bribery Adultery and lyes,   115
Where is the nation, I can't parallize.
With usury, extortion and oppression,
These be the *Hydraes*[26] of my stout transgression.
These be the bitter fountains, heads and roots,
Whence flow'd the source, the sprigs, the boughs
                    & fruits   120

21 **Belzebub:** Satan
22 **nick-names:** names such as "Puritans"
23 **Edwards youth:** another reference to Richard III's alleged murder of
his two nephews, who were sons of Edward IV
24 **Clarence hapless son:** George, Duke of Clarence, who was executed in
the Tower of London in 1478 and whose son Edward was also executed in 1499
25 **Jane:** Lady Jane Grey, a Protestant who, in accordance with Edward VI's
will, reigned for nine days in 1553 when she was only fifteen years old before
being executed by Queen Mary in 1554
26 **Hydraes:** mythological poisonous water snakes with many heads, which
would regrow after being severed

Of more then thou canst hear or I relate,
That with high hand I still did perpetrate:
For these were threatned the wofull day,
I mockt the Preachers, put it far away;
The Sermons yet upon Record do stand   125
That cri'd destruction to my wicked land:
I then believ'd not, now I feel and see,
The plague of stubborn incredulity.
Some lost their livings, some in prison pent,
Some fin'd, from house & friends to exile went.   130
Their silent tongues to heaven did vengeance cry,
Who saw their wrongs, & hath judg'd righteously
And will repay it seven-fold in my lap:
This is fore-runner of my Afterclap.
Nor took I warning by my neighbours falls,   135
I saw sad *Germanyes* dismantled walls,[27]
I saw her people famish'd, Nobles slain,
Her fruitfull land, a barren Heath remain.
I saw unmov'd, her Armyes foil'd and fled,
Wives forc'd, babes toss'd, her houses calcined.   140
I saw strong *Rochel*[28] yielded to her Foe,
Thousands of starved Christians there also.
I saw poor *Ireland*[29] bleeding out her last,
Such crueltyes as all reports have past;
Mine heart obdurate stood not yet agast.   145
Now sip I of that cup, and just't may be
The bottome dreggs reserved are for me.

New-England.

To all you've said, sad Mother I assent,
Your fearfull sins great cause there's to lament,

27 **Germanyes dismantled walls:** Thirty Years' War (1618–1648), which
was fueled by conflict between Protestants and Catholics
28 **Rochel:** La Rochelle, a stronghold of French Huguenots, who were
defeated in 1628
29 **Ireland:** Irish Insurrection of 1641

My guilty hands in part, hold up with you,   150
A Sharer in your punishment's my due.
But all you say amounts to this effect,
Not what you feel, but what you do expect,
Pray in plain terms, what is your present grief?
Then let's joyn heads & hearts for your relief.   155

Old England.

Well to the matter then, there's grown of late
'Twixt King and Peers a Question of State,
Which is the chief, the Law, or else the King.
One said, it's he, the other no such thing.
'Tis said, my beter part in Parliament   160
To ease my groaning Land, shew'd their intent,
To crush the proud, and right to each man deal,
To help the Church, and stay the Common-weal.
So many Obstacles came in their way,
As puts me to a stand what I should say;   165
Old customes, new Prerogatives stood on,
Had they not held Law fast, all had been gone:
Which by their prudence stood them in such stead
They took high *Strafford*[30] lower by the head.
And to their *Laud*[31] be't spoke, they held i'th tower   170
All *Englands* Metropolitane that hour;
This done, an act they would have passed fain,
No Prelate should his Bishoprick retain;
Here tugg'd they hard (indeed,) for all men saw
This must be done by Gospel, not by Law.   175
Next the Militia they urged sore,
This was deny'd, (I need not say wherefore)
The King displeas'd at *York*,[32] himself absents,
They humbly beg return, shew their intents;

30 **Strafford:** Thomas Wentworth, Earl of Strafford and minister of Charles I, who was executed in 1641
31 **Laud:** William Laud, Archbishop of Canterbury, who was imprisoned and later executed in 1645
32 **York:** place where Charles I established his headquarters during the civil war

The writing, printing, posting too and fro,   180
Shews all was done, I'le therefore let it go.
But now I come to speak of my disaster,
Contention grown, 'twixt Subjects & their Master;
They worded it so long, they fell to blows,
That thousands lay on heaps, here bleeds my woes,   185
I that no wars so many years have known,
Am now destroy'd and slaught'red by mine own;
But could the Field alone this strife decide,
One Battel two or three I might abide:
But these may be beginnings of more woe   190
Who knows, but this may be my overthrow.
Oh pity me in this sad perturbation,
My plundred Towns, my houses devastation,
My weeping Virgins and my young men slain;
My wealthy trading fall'n, my dearth of grain,   195
The seed-times come, but ploughman hath no hope
Because he knows not who shall inn his Crop:
The poor they want their pay, their children bread,
Their woful Mothers tears unpittied,
If any pity in thy heart remain,   200
Or any child-like love thou dost retain,
For my relief, do what there lyes in thee,
And recompence that good I've done to thee.

New England.

Dear Mother cease complaints & wipe your eyes,
Shake off your dust, chear up, and now arise,   205
You are my Mother Nurse, and I your flesh,
Your sunken bowels gladly would refresh,
Your griefs I pity, but soon hope to see,
Out of your troubles much good fruit to be;
To see those latter dayes of hop'd for good,   210
Though now beclouded all with tears and blood;
After dark Popery the day did clear,
But now the Sun in's brightness shall appear.
Blest be the Nobles of thy noble Land,

With ventur'd lives for Truths defence that stand. 215
Blest be thy Commons,[33] who for common good,
And thy infringed Laws have boldly stood.
Blest be thy Counties, who did aid thee still,
With hearts and States to testifie their will.
Blest be thy Preachers, who do chear thee on, 220
O cry the Sword of God, and *Gideon*;[34]
And shall I not on them wish *Mero*'s curse,[35]
That help thee not with prayers, Arms and purse?
And for my self let miseries abound,
If mindless of thy State I e're be found. 225
These are the dayes the Churches foes to crush,
To root out Popelings head, tail, branch and rush;
Let's bring *Baals* vestments forth to make a fire,
Their Mytires, Surplices, and all their Tire,
Copes, Rotchets, Crossiers,[36] and such empty trash, 230
And let their Names consume, but let the flash
Light Christendome, and all the world to see
We hate *Romes* whore,[37] with all her trumpery.
Go on brave *Essex*[38] with a Loyal heart,
Not false to King, nor to the better part; 235
But those that hurt his people and his Crown,
As duty binds, expel and tread them down.
And ye brave Nobles chase away all fear,
And to this hopeful Cause closely adhere;
O Mother can you weep, and have such Peers, 240
When they are gone, then drown your self in tears
If now you weep so much, that then no more
The briny Ocean will o'reflow your shore.

33 **Commons:** House of Commons
34 **O cry the Sword of God, and Gideon:** Judg. 7:18–20
35 **Mero's Curse:** Judg. 5:23
36 **Mytires, . . . Crossiers:** vestiges of formal worship in the Anglican Church
37 **Romes whore:** the Anglican Church, particularly in its emulation of Catholic practices
38 **Essex:** Robert Devereux, third Earl of Essex, who was a leader of the Parliamentary Army

These, these are they I trust, with *Charles* our King,
Out of all mists such glorious dayes shall bring;   245
That dazled eyes beholding much shall wonder
At that thy setled peace, thy wealth and splendor.
Thy Church and weal establish'd in such manner,
That all shall joy, that thou display'dst thy Banner;
And discipline erected so I trust,   250
That nursing Kings shall come and lick thy dust:
The Justice shall in all thy Courts take place,
Without respect of person, or of case;
Then Bribes shall cease, & Suits shall not stick long
Patience and purse of Clients oft to wrong: 255
Then high Commissions shall fall to decay,
And Pursivants, and Catchpoles[39] want their pay.
So shall thy happy Nation ever flourish,
When truth & righteousnes they thus shall nourish
When thus in peace, thine Armies brave send out,   260
To sack proud *Rome*,[40] and all her Vassals rout;
There let thy Name, thy fame, and glory shine,
As did thine Ancestors in *Palestine*:
And let her spoyls full pay, with Interest be,
Of what unjustly once she poll'd from thee.   265
Of all the woes thou canst, let her be sped,
And on her pour the vengeance threatned;
Bring forth the Beast that rul'd the World with's beck,
And tear his flesh, & set your feet on's neck;
And make his filthy Den so desolate,   270
To th' stonishment of all that knew his state:
This done with brandish'd Swords to *Turky* goe,[41]
For then what is't, but English blades dare do,
And lay her waste for so's the sacred Doom,
And do to *Gog*[42] as thou hast done to *Rome*.   275

39 **Pursivants, and Catchpoles:** officers of the court
40 **sack proud Rome:** Bradstreet's desire that the army might vanquish
Catholic Rome
41 **to Turky goe:** her further suggestion that the army might then conquer
Islamic Turkey
42 **Gog:** Ezek. 38–39, Rev. 20:8

Oh *Abraham*'s seed[43] lift up your heads on high,
For sure the day of your Redemption's nigh;
The Scales shall fall from your long blinded eyes,
And him you shall adore who now despise,
Then fulness of the Nations in shall flow,   280
And Jew and Gentile to one worship go;
Then follows dayes of happiness and rest;
Whose lot doth fall, to live therein is blest:
No Canaanite shall then be found i'th' Land,
And holiness on horses bells[44] shall stand.   285
If this make way thereto, then sigh no more,
But if at all, thou didst not see't before;
Farewel dear Mother, rightest cause prevail,
And in a while, you'le tell another tale.

Even though Queen Elizabeth I died almost a decade before Bradstreet was born, Bradstreet considered her a per-
sonally inspiring figure of political prowess and remarkable
strength. In the following poem, she celebrates Elizabeth's
multifaceted greatness among monarchs of all time and countries. Although Bradstreet notes it is impossible to chronicle
all of Elizabeth's accomplishments, she highlights such feats as
peace and prosperity in England, subjugation of foreign foes,
and successful exploration. She compares Elizabeth to other
women rulers and concludes that she has no match.

Most interesting to recent critics, Bradstreet uses the
poem to catapult into a declaration of women's capabilities
and worth. She notes that the demeaning of women's men-

43 **Abraham's seed:** Gal. 3:29
44 **No Canaanite . . . holiness on horses bells:** Zech. 14:20–21

4.1 Autograph of Elizabeth I.

tal capacities, a common phenomenon in Bradstreet's time, would have been treasonous in the case of Queen Elizabeth.

In Honour of that High and Mighty Princess Queen Elizabeth of Happy Memory.

The Proeme.[45]

> Although great Queen thou now in silence lye
> Yet thy loud Herald Fame doth to the sky
> Thy wondrous worth proclaim in every Clime,
> And so hath vow'd while there is world or time.
> So great's thy glory and thine excellence,   5
> The sound thereof rapts every humane sence,
> That men account it no impiety,
> To say thou wert a fleshly Diety:
> Thousands bring offerings (though out of date)
> Thy world of honours to accumulate,   10
> 'Mongst hundred Hecatombs[46] of roaring verse,
> Mine bleating stands before thy royal Herse.
> Thou never didst nor canst thou now disdain
> T' accept the tribute of a loyal brain.
> Thy clemency did yerst esteem as much   15

45 **Proeme:** a preface
46 **Hecatombs:** in ancient Greece and Rome, sacrifices of 100 oxen at a time

The acclamations of the poor as rich,
Which makes me deem my rudeness is no wrong,
Though I resound thy praises 'mongst the throng.

The Poem.

No *Phœnix* pen,[47] nor *Spencers* poetry,
No *Speeds* nor *Cambdens* learned History,[48]   20
Elizahs works, warrs, praise, can e're compact,
The World's the Theatre where she did act.
No memoryes nor volumes can contain
The 'leven Olympiads[49] of her happy reign:
Who was so good, so just, so learn'd so wise,   25
From all the Kings on earth she won the prize.
Nor say I more then duly is her due,
Millions will testifie that this is true.
She hath wip'd off th' aspersion of her Sex,
That women wisdome lack to play the Rex: 30
Spains Monarch,[50] sayes not so, nor yet his host:
She taught them better manners, to their cost.
The *Salique* law,[51] in force now had not been,
If *France* had ever hop'd for such a Queen.
But can you Doctors now this point dispute,   35
She's Argument enough to make you mute.
Since first the sun did run his nere run race,
And earth had once a year, a new old face,
Since time was time, and man unmanly man,
Come shew me such a *Phœnix* if you can?   40

47 **Phoenix pen:** reference to the works of Sir Philip Sidney (1554–1586),
to whom *The Phoenix Nest* (1593), a collection of poetry by various writers, was
dedicated
48 **Spencers poetry, . . . Cambdens learned History:** Edmund Spenser
(c.1552–1599), who wrote *The Faerie Queene*, an allegory in which the
character Gloriana represents Queen Elizabeth; John Speed (1552–1629) and
William Camden (1551–1623), who were British historians
49 **'leven Olympiads:** Elizabeth's reign from 1558 to 1603
50 **Spains Monarch:** King Philip II
51 **Salique law:** the law governing the Salian Franks, who did not allow
women to rule

Was ever people better rul'd then hers?
Was ever land more happy freed from stirrs?
Did ever wealth in *England* more abound?
Her victoryes in forreign Coasts resound,
Ships more invincible then *Spain's,* her foe   45
She wrackt, she sackt, she sunk his Armado:[52]
Her stately troops advanc'd to *Lisbons* wall
Don Anthony[53] in's right there to install.
She frankly helpt, *Franks* brave distressed King,
The States united now her fame do sing,   50
She their Protectrix was, they well do know
Unto our dread Virago,[54] what they owe.
Her Nobles sacrific'd their noble blood,
Nor men nor Coyn she spar'd to do them good.
The rude untamed *Irish,* she did quel,   55
Before her picture the proud *Tyrone*[55] fell.
Had ever prince such Counsellours as she?
Her self *Minerva*[56] caus'd them so to be.
Such Captains and such souldiers never seen,
As were the Subjects of our *Pallas*[57] Queen.   60
Her Sea-men through all straights the world did round;
Terra incognita[58] might know the sound.
Her *Drake*[59] came laden home with Spanish gold:
Her *Essex*[60] took *Cades,* their Herculean Hold:

52 **sunk his Armado:** Elizabeth's sinking of the Spanish Armada in 1588
53 **Don Anthony:** Don Antonio (1531–1595), who claimed the throne of Portugal, then sought refuge in England and was used by Elizabeth to instigate trouble against Spain under Philip II
54 **Virago:** a strong woman
55 **Tyrone:** Hugh O'Neill, second Earl of Tyrone (c.1540–1616), an Irish chieftain with whom Elizabeth successfully resolved hostilities
56 **Minerva:** in Roman myth, the goddess of defensive war, the arts, and wisdom
57 **Pallas:** Pallas Athena, who in Greek mythology was the goddess of judicious war, the arts, and wisdom
58 **Terra incognita:** an unexplored area
59 **Drake:** Sir Francis Drake (c. 1540–1596), who was the first English person to sail around the world and who brought home much plunder for Elizabeth
60 **Essex:** Robert Devereux, the second Earl of Essex (1567–1601), who was a favorite of Elizabeth and who led the invasion of Cadiz, Spain

But time would fail me, so my tongue would to,   65
To tell of half she did, or she could doe.
Semiramis[61] to her, is but obscure,
More infamy then fame, she did procure.
She built her glory but on *Babels* walls,
Worlds wonder for a while, but yet it falls.   70
Fierce *Tomris*,[62] (*Cyrus* heads-man) *Scythians* queen,
Had put her harness off, had shee but seen
Our Amazon in th' Camp of *Tilbury*,[63]
Judging all valour and all Majesty
Within that Princess to have residence,   75
And prostrate yielded to her excellence.
Dido[64] first Foundress of proud *Carthage* walls,
(Who living consummates her Funeralls)
A great *Eliza*, but compar'd with ours,
How vanisheth her glory, wealth and powers.   80
Profuse, proud *Cleopatra*,[65] whose wrong name,
Instead of glory, prov'd her Countryes shame:
Of her what worth in Storyes to be seen,
But that she was a rich Egyptian Queen.
Zenobya[66] potent Empress of the East,   85
And of all these, without compare the best,
Whom none but great *Aurelius*[67] could quel;
Yet for our Queen is no fit Parallel.
She was a Phœnix Queen, so shall she be,
Her ashes not reviv'd, more Phœnix she.   90
Her personal perfections, who would tell,
Must dip his pen in th' *Heleconian Well*,[68]

61 **Semiramis:** legendary wife of Nimrod and queen of Assyria
62 **Tomris:** Queen Tomyris of the Massagetai, who defeated the Persian
King Cyrus
63 **Tilbury:** place where Elizabeth inspected her troops in 1588
64 **Dido:** legendary queen of Carthage, who in Virgil's *Aeneid* fell in love
with Aeneas and committed suicide when he deserted her
65 **Cleopatra:** queen of Ancient Egypt
66 **Zenobya:** Queen Zenobia, who ruled Palmyra, a city state in Syria
67 **Aurelius:** Roman Emperor Marcus Aurelius, who conquered Britain
68 **Heleconian Well:** water from the streams of Helicon, a mountain in
central Greece considered to be the abode of the muses in Greek myth

Which I may not, my pride doth but aspire
To read what others write, and so admire.
Now say, have women worth? or have they none? 95
Or had they some, but with our Queen is't gone?
Nay Masculines, you have thus taxt us long,
But she, though dead, will vindicate our wrong.
Let such as say our Sex is void of Reason,
Know tis a Slander now, but once was Treason. 100
But happy *England* which had such a Queen;
Yea happy, happy, had those dayes still been:
But happiness lyes in a higher sphere,
Then wonder not *Eliza* moves not here.
Full fraught with honour, riches and with dayes 105
She set, she set, like *Titan*[69] in his raves.
Nor more shall rise or set so glorious sun
Untill the heavens great revolution,
If then new things their old forms shall retain,
Eliza shall rule *Albion*[70] once again. 110

Her Epitaph.

Here sleeps THE Queen, this is the Royal Bed,
Of th' Damask Rose, sprung from the white and red,[71]
Whose sweet perfume fills the all-filling Air:
This Rose is wither'd, once so lovely fair.
On neither tree did grow such Rose before, 115
The greater was our gain, our loss the more.

Another.

Here lyes the pride of Queens, Pattern of Kings,
So blaze it Fame, here's feathers for thy wings.
Here lyes the envi'd, yet unparalled Prince,

69 **Titan:** in Greek myth, a giant who helped to rule the world
70 **Albion:** ancient Latin term for England
71 **sprung from the white and red:** the House of Tudor, which united
the Houses of York and Lancaster

Whose living virtues speak, (though dead long since)   120
If many worlds, as that Fantastick fram'd,
In every one be her great glory fam'd.

Many contemporary critics view this poem, with its skill-ful use of nature images, as one of Bradstreet's best. Her first-person speaker achieves a delicate balance in her con-templations between a celebration of nature's beauty and nature's inherent praise of its creator on the one hand and a recognition of the effects of the fall, particularly on hu-mankind, on the other. The poem alternates between almost romantic visions of nature, especially the sun and streams, and stark portraits of the depraved aftermath of Adam's fall, including Cain's murder of Abel.

Ultimately, Bradstreet checks her celebration of nature and its capacity for self-renewal by noting in stanza 20 that only humans experience eternity. She asserts in stan-zas 32 and 33 that humans often vainly look to worldly pleasures for satisfaction, though eternity offers the only true security possible. Although some critics characterize the poem as lacking unity, Bradstreet's presentation of a suc-cession of images reflects the fluid thought processes of its speaker—a contemplative person.

Contemplations.

1

Some time now past in the Autumnal Tide,
When *Phœbus*[72] wanted but one hour to bed,
The trees all richly clad, yet void of pride,

72 **Phoebus:** the Greek personification of the sun

Where gilded o're by his rich golden head.
Their leaves & fruits seem'd painted, but was true   5
Of green, of red, of yellow, mixed hew,
Rapt were my sences at this delectable view.

2

I wist not what to wish, yet sure thought I,
If so much excellence abide below;
How excellent is he that dwells on high?   10
Whose power and beauty by his works we know.
Sure he is goodness, wisdome, glory, light,
That hath this under world so richly dight:
More Heaven then Earth was here no winter &
            no night.

3

Then on a stately Oak I cast mine Eye,   15
Whose ruffling top the Clouds seem'd to aspire;
How long since thou wast in thine Infancy?
Thy strength, and stature, more thy years admire,
Hath hundred winters past since thou wast born?
Or thousand since thou brakest thy shell of horn,   20
If so, all these as nought, Eternity doth scorn.

4

Then higher on the glistering Sun I gaz'd,
Whose beams was shaded by the leavie Tree,
The more I look'd, the more I grew amaz'd,
And softly said, what glory's like to thee?   25
Soul of this world, this Universes Eye,
No wonder, some made thee a Deity:
Had I not better known, (alas) the same had I.

5

Thou as a Bridegroom from thy Chamber rushes,
And as a strong man, joyes to run a race,   30
The morn doth usher thee, with smiles & blushes,
The Earth reflects her glances in thy face.
Birds, insects, Animals with Vegative,
Thy heat from death and dulness doth revive:
And in the darksome womb of fruitful nature dive.   35

6

Thy swift Annual, and diurnal Course,
Thy daily streight, and yearly oblique path,
Thy pleasing fervor, and thy scorching force,
All mortals here the feeling knowledg hath.
Thy presence makes it day, thy absence night,   40
Quaternal Seasons caused by thy might:
Hail Creature, full of sweetness, beauty & delight.

7

Art thou so full of glory, that no Eye
Hath strength, thy shining Rayes once to behold?
And is thy splendid Throne erect so high?   45
As to approach it, can no earthly mould.
How full of glory then must thy Creator be?
Who gave this bright light luster unto thee:
Admir'd, ador'd for ever, be that Majesty.

8

Silent alone, where none or saw, or heard,   50
In pathless paths I lead my wandring feet,

My humble Eyes to lofty Skyes I rear'd
To sing some Song, my mazed Muse thought meet.
My great Creator I would magnifie,
That nature had, thus decked liberally: 55
But Ah, and Ah, again, my imbecility!

9

I heard the merry grashopper then sing,
The black clad Cricket, bear a second part,
They kept one tune, and plaid on the same string,
Seeming to glory in their little Art.   60
Shall Creatures abject, thus their voices raise?
And in their kind resound their makers praise:
Whilst I as mute, can warble forth no higher layes.

10

When present times look back to Ages past,
And men in being fancy those are dead,   65
It makes things gone perpetually to last,
And calls back moneths and years that long since fled
It makes a man more aged in conceit,
Than was *Methuselah*,[73] or's grand-sire great:
While of their persons & their acts his mind doth treat.   70

11

Sometimes in *Eden* fair, he seems to be,
Sees glorious *Adam* there made Lord of all,
Fancyes the Apple, dangle on the Tree,
That turn'd his Sovereign to a naked thral.
Who like a miscreant's driven from that place,   75
To get his bread with pain, and sweat of face:
A penalty impos'd on his backsliding Race.

73 **Methuselah:** the son of Enoch who lived 969 years (Gen. 5:21–27)

12

Here sits our Grandame in retired place,
And in her lap, her bloody *Cain* new born,
The weeping Imp oft looks her in the face,   80
Bewails his unknown hap, and fate forlorn;
His Mother sighs, to think of Paradise,
And how she lost her bliss, to be more wise,
Believing him that was, and is, Father of lyes.

13

Here *Cain* and *Abel* come to sacrfiice,   85
Fruits of the Earth, and Fatlings each do bring,
On *Abels* gift the fire descends from Skies,
But no such sign on false *Cain's* offering;
With sullen hateful looks he goes his wayes.
Hath thousand thoughts to end his brothers dayes,   90
Upon whose blood his future good he hopes to raise

14

There *Abel* keeps his sheep, no ill he thinks,
His brother comes, then acts his fratricide,
The Virgin Earth, of blood her first draught drinks
But since that time she often hath been cloy'd;   95
The wretch with gastly face and dreadful mind,
Thinks each he sees will serve him in his kind,
Though none on Earth but kindred near then could he find.

15

Who fancyes not his looks now at the Barr,
His face like death, his heart with horror fraught,   100
Nor Male-factor ever felt like warr,
When deep dispair, with wish of life hath sought,

Branded with guilt, and crusht with treble woes,
A Vagabond to Land of *Nod*[74] he goes.
A City builds, that wals might him secure from foes.   105

16

Who thinks not oft upon the Fathers ages.
Their long descent, how nephews sons they saw,
The starry observations of those Sages,
And how their precepts to their sons were law,
How Adam sigh'd to see his Progeny,   110
Cloath'd all in his black sinfull Livery,
Who neither guilt, nor yet the punishment could fly.

17

Our Life compare we with their length of dayes
Who to the tenth of theirs doth now arrive?
And though thus short, we shorten many wayes,   115
Living so little while we are alive;
In eating, drinking, sleeping, vain delight
So unawares comes on perpetual night,
And puts all pleasures vain unto eternal flight.

18

When I behold the heavens as in their prime,   120
And then the earth (though old) stil clad in green,
The stones and trees, insensible of time,
Nor age nor wrinkle on their front are seen;
If winter come, and greeness then do fade,
A Spring returns, and they more youthfull made;   125
But Man grows old, lies down, remains where once he's laid.

---

74 **Nod:** place east of Eden where Cain settled after killing Abel (Gen. 4:16)

20 [19]

By birth more noble than those creatures all,
Yet seems by nature and by custome curs'd,
No sooner born, but grief and care makes fall
That state obliterate he had at first: 130
Nor youth, nor strength, nor wisdom spring again
Nor habitations long their names retain,
But in oblivion to the final day remain.

20

Shall I then praise the heavens, the trees, the earth
Because their beauty and their strength last longer   135
Shall I wish there, or never to had birth,
Because they're bigger, and their bodyes stronger?
Nay, they shall darken, perish, fade and dye,
And when unmade, so ever shall they lye,
But man was made for endless immortality.   140

21

Under the cooling shadow of a stately Elm
Close sate I by a goodly Rivers side,
Where gliding streams the Rocks did overwhelm;
A lonely place, with pleasures dignifi'd.
I once that lov'd the shady woods so well,   145
Now thought the rivers did the trees excel,
And if the sun would ever shine, there would I dwell.

22

While on the stealing stream I fixt mine eye,
Which to the long'd for Ocean held its course,
I markt, nor crooks, nor rubs that there did lye   150
Could hinder ought, but still augment its force:

O happy Flood, quoth I, that holds thy race
Till thou arrive at thy beloved place,
Nor is it rocks or shoals that can obstruct thy pace

23

Nor is't enough, that thou alone may'st slide,   155
But hundred brooks in thy cleer waves do meet,
So hand in hand along with thee they glide
To *Thetis*[75] house, where all imbrace and greet:
Thou Emblem true, of what I count the best,
O could I lead my Rivolets to rest,   160
So may we press to that vast mansion, ever blest.

24

Ye Fish which in this liquid Region 'bide,
That for each season, have your habitation,
Now salt, now fresh where you think best to glide
To unknown coasts to give a visitation,   165
In Lakes and ponds, you leave your numerous fry,
So nature taught, and yet you know not why,
You watry folk that know not your felicity.

25

Look how the wantons frisk to tast the air,
Then to the colder bottome streight they dive,   170
Eftsoon to *Neptun*'s glassie Hall[76] repair
To see what trade they great ones there do drive,
Who forrage o're the spacious sea-green field,
And take the trembling prey before it yield,
Whose armour is their scales, their spreading fins
            their shield.   175

75 **Thetis:** the Greek personification of the sea and the mother of Achilles
76 **Neptun's glassie Hall:** the sea, the habitation of Neptune; Roman
personification of the sea

26

While musing thus with contemplation fed,
And thousand fancies buzzing in my brain,
The sweet-tongu'd Philomel[77] percht ore my head,
And chanted forth a most melodious strain
Which rapt me so with wonder and delight,   180
I judg'd my hearing better then my sight,
And wisht me wings with her a while to take my flight.

28 [27]

O merry Bird (said I) that fears no snares,
That neither toyles nor hoards up in thy barn,
Feels no sad thoughts, nor cruciating cares   185
To gain more good, or shun what might thee harm
Thy cloaths ne're wear, thy meat is every where,
Thy bed a bough, thy drink the water cleer,
Reminds not what is past, nor whats to come dost fear

28

The dawning morn with songs thou dost prevent,   190
Sets hundred notes unto thy feathered crew,
So each one tunes his pretty instrument,
And warbling out the old, begin anew,
And thus they pass their youth in summer season,
Then follow thee into a better Region,   195
where winter's never felt by that sweet airy legion

29

Man at the best a creature frail and vain,
In knowledg ignorant, in strength but weak,
Subject to sorrows, losses, sickness, pain,

77 **Philomel:** the nightingale

Each storm his state, his mind, his body break,   200
From some of these he never finds cessation,
But day or night, within, without, vexation,
Troubles from foes, from friends, from dearest, near'st
    Relation

30

And yet this sinfull creature, frail and vain,
This lump of wretchedness, of sin and sorrow,   205
This weather-beaten vessel wrackt with pain,
Joyes not in hope of an eternal morrow;
Nor all his losses, crosses and vexation,
In weight, in frequency and long duration
Can make him deeply groan for that divine Translation. 210

31

The Mariner that on smooth waves doth glide,
Sings merrily, and steers his Barque with ease,
As if he had command of wind and tide,
And now become great Master of the seas;
But suddenly a storm spoiles all the sport,   215
And makes him long for a more quiet port,
Which 'gainst all adverse winds may serve for fort.

32

So he that saileth in this world of pleasure,
Feeding on sweets, that never bit of th' sowre,
That's full of friends, of honour and of treasure,   220
Fond fool, he takes this earth ev'n for heav'ns bower.
But sad affliction comes and makes him see
Here's neither honour, wealth, nor safety;
Only above is found all with security.

33

O Time the fatal wrack of mortal things,   225
That draws oblivions curtains over kings,
Their sumptuous monuments, men know them not,
Their names without a Record are forgot,
Their parts, their ports, their pomp's all laid in th' dust
Nor wit nor gold, nor buildings scape times rust;   230
But he whose name is grav'd in the white stone[78]
Shall last and shine when all of these are gone.

Here Bradstreet offers a rhymed couplet paraphrase of
the Geneva Bible's rendering of 2 Samuel 1:19–27. Although she regularly takes up biblical themes and motifs,
such a close and extended paraphrase is not common
among her surviving work.

Davids Lamentation for Saul and Jonathan.

2. Sam. 1. 19.

Alas slain is the Head of Israel,
Illustrious *Saul* whose beauty did excell,
Upon thy places mountainous and high,
How did the Mighty fall, and falling dye?
In *Gath* let not this thing be spoken on,   5
Nor published in streets of *Askalon*,
Lest daughters of the Philistines rejoyce,
Lest the uncircumcis'd lift up their voice.
O *Gilbo* Mounts, let never pearled dew,
Nor fruitfull showres your barren tops bestrew,   10

---

78 **white stone:** Rev. 2:17

Nor fields of offrings ever on you grow,
Nor any pleasant thing e're may you show;
For there the Mighty Ones did soon decay,
The shield of *Saul* was vilely cast away,
There had his dignity so sore a foyle,   15
As if his head ne're felt the sacred oyle.
Sometimes from crimson, bloody of gastly slain,
The bow of *Jonathan* ne're turn'd in vain:
Nor from the fat, and spoils of Mighty men
With bloodless sword did *Saul* turn back agen.   20
Pleasant and lovely, were they both in life,
And in their death was found no parting strife.
Swifter then swiftest Eagles so were they,
Stronger then Lions ramping for their prey.
O Israels Dames, o'reflow your beauteous eyes   25
For valiant *Saul* who on Mount *Gilbo* lyes,
Who cloathed you in Cloath of richest Dye,
And choice delights, full of variety,
On your array put ornaments of gold,
Which made you yet more beauteous to behold.   30
O! how in Battle did the mighty fall
In midst of strength not succoured at all.
O lovely *Jonathan!* how wast thou slain?
In places high, full low thou didst remain.
Distrest for thee I am, dear *Jonathan*,   35
Thy love was wonderfull, surpassing man,
Exceeding all the love that's Feminine,
So pleasant hast thou been, dear brother mine,
How are the mighty fall'n into decay?
And warlike weapons perished away?   40

Bradstreet again uses rhymed couplets to consider biblical concepts. Here, however, she does not paraphrase closely

but instead employs her own first-person speaker in order to agree with Solomon as he expresses the overarching theme of Ecclesiastes—the vanity of life—and to contrast such vanity with the perfection of the new Jerusalem as described in Revelation 21–22. Dismissing the Stoic notion that it is possible to live impassively, Bradstreet acknowledges the validity of human emotion when confronted with the vanity of life, although she ultimately directs herself to meditate on the heavenly state when overwhelmed by such vanity. In her assertions about the fleeting nature of power and position, she directly references the imprisonment of Charles I, "now a captive, that was King of late."

The Vanity of all worldly things.

As he said vanity, so vain say I,
Oh! vanity, O vain all under Sky;
Where is the man can say, lo I have found
On brittle Earth a Consolation sound?
What is't in honour to be set on high?   5
No, they like Beasts and Sons of men shall dye:
And whil'st they live, how oft doth turn their fate,
He's now a captive, that was King of late.
What is't in wealth, great Treasures to obtain?
No, that's but labour, anxious care and pain,   10
He heaps up riches, and he heaps up sorrow,
It's his to day, but who's his heir to morrow?
What then? Content in pleasures canst thou find,
More vain then all, that's but to grasp the wind.
The sensual senses for a time they please,   15
Mean while the conscience rage, who shall appease?
What is't in beauty? No that's but a snare,
They're foul enough to day, that once were fair.
What is't in flowring youth, or manly age?
The first is prone to vice, the last to rage.   20

Where is it then, in wisdom, learning arts?
Sure if on earth, it must be in those parts:
Yet these the wisest man of men did find
But vanity, vexation of mind.
And he that knowes the most, doth still bemoan   25
He knows not all that here is to be known.
What is it then, to doe as *Stoicks* tell,
Nor laugh, nor weep, let things go ill or well.
Such *Stoicks* are but Stocks such teaching vain,
While man is man, he shall have ease or pain.   30
If not in honour, beauty, age nor treasure,
Nor yet in learning, wisdome, youth nor pleasure,
Where shall I climb, sound, seek search or find
That *Summum Bonum* which may stay my mind?
There is a path, no vultures eye hath seen,   35
Where Lion fierce, nor lions whelps have been,
Which leads unto that living Chrystal Fount,
Who drinks thereof, the world doth nought account
The depth & sea have said tis not in me,
With pearl and gold, it shall not valued be.   40
For Saphire, Onix, Topaz who would change:
Its hid from eyes of men, they count it strange.
Death and destruction the same hath heard,
But where & what it is, from heaven's declar'd,
It brings to honour, which shall ne're decay,   45
It stores with wealth which time can't wear away.
It yieldeth pleasures far beyond conceit,
And truly beautifies without deceit,
Nor strength, nor wisdome nor fresh youth shall fade
Nor death shall see, but are immortal made.   50
This pearl of price, this tree of life, this spring
Who is possessed of, shall reign a King.
Nor change of state, nor cares shall ever see,
But wear his crown unto eternity:
This satiates the Soul, this stayes the mind,   55
And all the rest, but Vanity we find.

Here Bradstreet employs both rhymed couplets and spirited dialogue in order to personify the struggle between the flesh and the spirit as expressed by Paul in passages such as Romans 7–8. Like "The Vanity of all worldly things," this poem underscores the role of contemplation in combating the flesh and presents a focus on eternity, as described in Revelation 21–22, as an antidote to carnal desires.

The Flesh and the Spirit.

In secret place where once I stood
Close by the Banks of *Lacrim* flood[79]
I heard two sisters reason on
Things that are past, and things to come;
One flesh was call'd, who had her eye   5
On worldly wealth and vanity;
The other Spirit, who did rear
Her thoughts unto a higher sphere:
Sister, quoth Flesh, what liv'st thou on
Nothing but Meditation?   10
Doth Contemplation feed thee so
Regardlesly to let earth goe?
Can Speculation satisfy
Notion without Reality?
Dost dream of things beyond the Moon   15
And dost thou hope to dwell there soon?
Hast treasures there laid up in store
That all in th' world thou count'st but poor?
Art fancy sick, or turn'd a Sot
To catch at shadowes which are not?   20
Come, come, Ile shew unto thy sence,

79 **Lacrim flood:** a river of tears

Industry hath its recompence.
What canst desire, but thou maist see
True substance in variety?
Dost honour like? acquire the same,   25
As some to their immortal fame:
And trophyes to thy name erect
Which wearing time shall ne're deject.
For riches dost thou long full sore?
Behold enough of precious store.   30
Earth hath more silver, pearls and gold,
Then eyes can see, or hands can hold.
Affect's thou pleasure? take thy fill,
Earth hath enough of what you will.
Then let not goe, what thou maist find,   35
For things unknown, only in mind.
Spir. Be still thou unregenerate part,
Disturb no more my setled heart,
For I have vow'd, (and so will doe)
Thee as a foe, still to pursue.   40
And combate with thee will and must,
Untill I see thee laid in th' dust.
Sisters we are, ye twins we be,
Yet deadly feud 'twixt thee and me;
For from one father are we not,   45
Thou by old Adam wast begot,
But my arise is from above,
Whence my dear father I do love.
Thou speak'st me fair, but hat'st me sore,
Thy flatt'ring shews Ile trust no more.   50
How oft thy slave, hast thou me made,
when I believ'd, what thou hast said,
And never had more cause of woe
Then when I did what thou bad'st doe.
Ile stop mine ears at these thy charms,   55
And count them for my deadly harms.
Thy sinfull pleasures I doe hate,
Thy riches are to me no bait,

Thine honours doe, nor will I love;
For my ambition lyes above.   60
My greatest honour it shall be
When I am victor over thee,
And triumph shall, with laurel head,
When thou my Captive shalt be led,
How I do live, thou need'st not scoff,   65
For I have meat thou know'st not off;
The hidden Manna I doe eat,
The word of life it is my meat.
My thoughts do yield me more content
Then can thy hours in pleasure spent.   70
Nor are they shadows which I catch,
Nor fancies vain at which I snatch,
But reach at things that are so high,
Beyond thy dull Capacity;
Eternal substance I do see,   75
With which inriched I would be:
Mine Eye doth pierce the heavens, and see
What is Invisible to thee.
My garments are not silk nor gold,
Nor such like trash which Earth doth hold,   80
But Royal Robes I shall have on,
More glorious then the glistring Sun;
My Crown not Diamonds, Pearls, and gold,
But such as Angels heads infold.
The City where I hope to dwell,   85
There's none on Earth can parallel;
The stately Walls both high and strong,
Are made of pretious *Jasper* stone;
The Gates of Pearl, both rich and clear,
And Angels are for Porters there;   90
The Streets thereof transparent gold,
Such as no Eye did e're behold,
A Chrystal River there doth run,
Which doth proceed from the Lambs Throne:
Of Life, there are the waters sure,   95

115

Which shall remain for ever pure,
Nor Sun, nor Moon, they have no need,
For glory doth from God proceed:
No Candle there, nor yet Torch light,
For there shall be no darksome night.   100
From sickness and infirmity,
For evermore they shall be free,
Nor withering age shall e're come there,
But beauty shall be bright and clear;
This City pure is not for thee,   105
For things unclean there shall not be:
If I of Heaven may have my fill,
Take thou the world, and all that will.

5

LOVER

Bradstreet's lasting love affair with her husband and her devoted relationships with her children and parents find expression in a number of her occasional poems. In these poems, she is clear about her deep-rooted attachment to her family members, yet she constantly recognizes God's overarching sovereignty in undergirding and ultimately preserving these relationships—whether on earth or in eternity.

Although early studies of the Puritans often portrayed them as a dour and loveless people, more recent scholarship has painted a much different picture. The following poem, in which Bradstreet describes an intimate relationship with her husband, Simon, helps to challenge previous stereotypes. True to form, Bradstreet not only celebrates the earthly delights of marriage but also brings in its eternal implications in her final lines.

To my Dear and loving Husband.

If ever two were one, then surely we.
If ever man were lov'd by wife, then thee;
If ever wife was happy in a man,
Compare with me ye women if you can.
I prize thy love more then whole Mines of gold,   5
Or all the riches that the East doth hold.
My love is such that Rivers cannot quench,
Nor ought but love from thee, give recompence.
Thy love is such I can no way repay,
The heavens reward thee manifold I pray.   10
Then while we live, in love lets so persever,
That when we live no more, we may live ever.

Many of Bradstreet's surviving love poems to Simon address her longing for him and her prayers for his safe travels as a representative of the young Massachusetts Bay Colony. In a number of these poems, Bradstreet employs a style similar to that of the metaphysical poets, using intricate and extended metaphors known as conceits. Here she describes the integral role Simon plays in her life with references to the human body. She also calls him her sun and likens their separation to the changing relationship between the sun and earth as winter comes and goes.

A Letter to her Husband, absent upon Publick employment.

My head, my heart, mine Eyes, my life, nay more,
My joy, my Magazine of earthly store,
If two be one, as surely thou and I,
How stayest thou there, whilst I at *Ipswich* lye?
So many steps, head from the heart to sever   5
If but a neck, soon should we be together:
I like the earth this season, mourn in black,
My Sun is gone so far in's Zodiack,
Whom whilst I 'joy'd, nor storms, nor frosts I felt,
His warmth such frigid colds did cause to melt.   10
My chilled limbs now nummed lye forlorn;
Return, return sweet *Sol* from *Capricorn*;
In this dead time, alas, what can I more
Then view those fruits which through thy heat I bore?
Which sweet contentment yield me for a space,   15
True living Pictures of their Fathers face.
O strange effect! now thou art *Southward* gone,
I weary grow, the tedious day so long;
But when thou *Northward* to me shalt return,
I wish my Sun may never set, but burn   20
Within the Cancer of my glowing breast,
The welcome house of him my dearest guest.
Where ever, ever stay, and go not thence,
Till natures sad decree shall call thee hence;
Flesh of thy flesh, bone of thy bone,   25
I here, thou there, yet both but one.

A. B.

5.1 Portrait of Bradstreet's husband, Simon, who served as governor of the colony following her death.

In "another" poetic letter to her husband during his absence, this one particularly effusive in its emotion, Bradstreet capitalizes on the sun motif. She implores Phoebus, the sun personified, to remind Simon of her anguish while he is absent and to implore him to return as soon as possible. She also compares Simon to the sun, able to dry up the "torrent" of despair she feels when he is gone.

Another.

Phoebus make haste, the day's too long, be gone,
The silent night's the fittest time for moan;
But stay this once, unto my suit give ear,
And tell my griefs in either Hemisphere:
(And if the whirling of thy wheels don't drown'd)   5
The woful accents of my doleful sound,
If in thy swift Carrier thou canst make stay,
I crave this boon, this Errand by the way,
Commend me to the man more lov'd than life,
Shew him the sorrows of his widdowed wife;   10
My dumpish thoughts, my groans, my brakish tears
My sobs, my longing hopes, my doubting fears,
And if he love, how can he there abide?
My Interest's more than all the world beside.
He that can tell the stars or Ocean sand,   15
Or all the grass that in the Meads do stand,
The leaves in th' woods, the hail or drops of rain,
Or in a corn-field number every grain,
Or every mote that in the sun-shine hops,
May count my sighs, and number all my drops: 20
Tell him, the countless steps that thou dost trace,
That once a day, thy Spouse thou mayst embrace;
And when thou canst not treat by loving mouth,
Thy rayes afar, salute her from the south.
But for one moneth I see no day (poor soul)   25
Like those far scituate under the pole,
Which day by day long wait for thy arise,
O how they joy when thou dost light the skyes.
O Phoebus, hadst thou but thus long from thine
Restrain'd the beams of thy beloved shine,   30
At thy return, if so thou could'st or durst
Behold a Chaos blacker then the first.
Tell him here's worse then a confused matter,
His little world's a fathom under water,

Nought but the fervor of his ardent beams   35
Hath power to dry the torrent of these streams.
Tell him I would say more, but cannot well,
Oppressed minds, abruptest tales do tell.
Now post with double speed, mark what I say,
By all our loves conjure him not to stay.   40

In yet another poetic letter to Simon during his absence, Bradstreet continues to give voice to her grief at their separation. She is perhaps more subtle in her expression than in the previous poem, employing the graceful yet compelling images of separated pairs of deer, turtle doves, and mullets to describe the companionship she and her husband share and to depict her intense longing for him.

Another.

As loving Hind that (Hartless) wants her Deer,
Scuds through the woods and Fern with harkning ear,
Perplext, in every bush & nook doth pry,
Her dearest Deer, might answer ear or eye;
So doth my anxious soul, which now doth miss,   5
A dearer Dear (far dearer Heart) then this.
Still wait with doubts, & hopes, and failing eye,
His voice to hear, or person to discry.
Or as the pensive Dove doth all alone
(On withered bough) most uncouthly bemoan   10
The absence of her Love, and loving Mate,
Whose loss hath made her so unfortunate:
Ev'n thus doe I, with many a deep sad groan
Bewail my turtle true, who now is gone,
His presence and his safe return, still wooes,   15

With thousand dolefull sighs & mournfull Cooes.
Or as the loving Mullet, that true Fish,
Her fellow lost, nor joy nor life do wish,
But lanches on that shore, there for to dye,
Where she her captive husband doth espy.   20
Mine being gone, I lead a joyless life,
I have a loving phere, yet seem no wife:
But worst of all, to him can't steer my course,
I here, he there, alas, both kept by force:
Return my Dear, my joy, my only Love,   25
Unto thy Hinde, thy Mullet and thy Dove,
Who neither joyes in pasture, house nor streams,
The substance gone, O me, these are but dreams.
Together at one Tree, oh let us brouze,
And like two Turtles roost within one house,   30
And like the Mullets in one River glide,
Let's still remain but one, till death divide.

Thy loving Love and Dearest Dear,
At home, abroad, and every where.

A. B.

Following the restoration of Charles II after the demise
of Cromwell's Commonwealth government, the Massachusetts Bay Colony found itself in a rather precarious situation. As a result, Simon Bradstreet and the Reverend
John Norton were commissioned by the colony to travel to
England to negotiate a new charter.

Here Bradstreet creates a poetic prayer to God, sup-
plicating for her husband's safety, yet framing her desires within those of the Almighty and promising that

she and Simon will serve him for the rest of their days upon his safe return.

Upon my dear and loving husband his goeing into England, Jan. 16, 1661.[1]

O thou most high who rulest All,
    And hear'st the Prayers of Thine;
O hearken, Lord, unto my suit,
    And my Petition signe.

Into thy everlasting Armes   5
    Of mercy I commend
Thy servant, Lord. Keep and preserve
    My husband, my dear freind.

At thy command, O Lord, he went,
    Nor nought could keep him back;   10
Then let thy promis joy his heart:
    O help, and bee not slack.

Uphold my heart in Thee, O God,
    Thou art my strenght and stay;
Thou see'st how weak and frail I am,   15
    Hide not thy face Away.

I, in obedience to thy Will,
    Thou knowest, did submitt;
It was my Duty so to doe,
    O Lord, accept of it.   20

Unthankfullnes for mercyes Past,
    Impute thou not to me;
O Lord, thou know'st my weak desire
    Was to sing Praise to Thee.

1 **Jan. 16, 1661:** Old Style dating, which would be 1662 according to New Style

Lord, bee thou Pilott to the ship,   25
    And send them prosperous gailes;
In stormes and sicknes, Lord, preserve.
    Thy Goodnes never failes.

Unto thy work he hath in hand,
    Lord, graunt Thou good Successe   30
And favour in their eyes, to whom
    He shall make his Addresse.

Remember, Lord, thy folk whom thou
    To wildernesse hast brought;
Let not thine own Inheritance   35
    Bee sold away for Nought.

But Tokens of thy favour Give—
    With Joy send back my Dear,
That I, and all thy servants, may
    Rejoice with heavenly chear.   40

Lord, let my eyes see once Again
    Him whom thou gavest me,
That wee together may sing Praise
    For ever unto Thee.

And the Remainder of oure Dayes   45
    Shall consecrated bee,
With an engaged heart to sing
    All Praises unto Thee.

Bradstreet and Norton returned safely to New England in the ship *Society* following their trip as emissaries to

Charles II. During their journey, rumors in the colony
had circulated that the two had been imprisoned, creat-
ing great consternation back home. Such rumors were un-
founded, as the two ambassadors had successfully negotiated an extension of their charter. Upon their return to
New England, they were not well received by all of the
Massachusetts Bay Colony residents, however, since they
had agreed to greater religious toleration in exchange for
the charter.

Here Bradstreet thanks God for answering the prayer of
her previous poem and seeks divine assistance in fulfilling
the vow she made.

In thankfull Remembrance for my dear husbands safe Arrivall Sept. 3, 1662.

What shall I render to thy Name,
    Or how thy Praises speak;
My thankes how shall I testefye?
    O Lord, thou know'st I'm weak.

I ow so much, so little can   5
    Return unto thy Name,
Confusion seases on my Soul,
    And I am fill'd with shame.

O thou that hearest Prayers, Lord,
    To Thee shall come all Flesh;   10
Thou hast me heard and answered,
    My 'Plaints have had accesse.

What did I ask for but thou gav'st?
    What could I more desire?
But Thankfullnes, even all my dayes,   15
    I humbly this Require.

Thy mercyes, Lord, have been so great,
   In number numberles,
Impossible for to recount
   Or any way expresse.   20

O help thy Saints that sought thy Face,
   T' Return unto thee Praise,
And walk before thee as they ought,
   In strict and upright wayes.

Although her subject is the peril of childbirth, Bradstreet presents in the following a love poem to her husband. In a time fraught with a high maternal and infant mortality rate, Bradstreet frames her love within the possibility of separation by death. She candidly expresses her fear of such separation, as well as her desire that her husband remember her in death and protect her children from mistreatment by a stepmother.

Before the Birth of one of her Children.

All things within this fading world hath end,
Adversity doth still our joyes attend;
No tyes so strong, no friends so dear and sweet,
But with deaths parting blow is sure to meet.
The sentence past is most irrevocable,   5
A common thing, yet oh inevitable;
How soon, my Dear, death may my steps attend,
How soon't may be thy Lot to lose thy friend,
We both are ignorant, yet love bids me
These farewell lines to recommend to thee,   10
That when that knot's unty'd that made us one,
I may seem thine, who in effect am none.

And if I see not half my dayes that's due,
What nature would, God grant to yours and you;
The many faults that well you know I have,   15
Let be interr'd in my oblivious grave;
If any worth or virtue were in me,
Let that live freshly in thy memory
And when thou feel'st no grief, as I no harms,
Yet love thy dead, who long lay in thine arms: 20
And when thy loss shall be repaid with gains
Look to my little babes my dear remains.
And if thou love thy self, or loved'st me
These O protect from step Dames injury.
And if chance to thine eyes shall bring this verse,   25
With some sad sighs honour my absent Herse;
And kiss this paper for thy loves dear sake,
Who with salt tears this last Farewel did take.

A. B.

In spite of her fears about the dangers of childbirth, as expressed in the previous poem, Bradstreet safely gave birth to eight children, seven of whom survived her. Here she describes her relationship with her children through the metaphor of a mother bird. This image has been captured in a stained glass window in St. Botolph's Church in Boston, Lincolnshire, England.

In reference to her Children, 23. June, 1656.[2]

I had eight birds hatcht in one nest,
Four Cocks there were, and Hens the rest,

2 **23. June, 1656:** original date of the poem, which critics note must be an error, for the poem describes events that transpired over a year after 1656

I nurst them up with pain and care,
Nor cost, nor labour did I spare,
Till at the last they felt their wing.   5
Mounted the Trees, and learn'd to sing;
Chief of the Brood[3] then took his flight,
To Regions far, and left me quite:
My mournful chirps I after send,
Till he return, or I do end,   10
Leave not thy nest, thy Dam and Sire,
Fly back and sing amidst this Quire.
My second bird[4] did take her flight,
And with her mate flew out of sight;
Southward they both their course did bend,   15
And Seasons twain they there did spend:
Till after blown by *Southern* gales,
They *Norward* steer'd with filled sayles.
A prettier bird was no where seen,
Along the Beach among the treen.   20
I have a third[5] of colour white,
On whom I plac'd no small delight;
Coupled with mate loving and true,
Hath also bid her Dam adieu:
And where *Aurora* first appears,   25
She now hath percht, to spend her years;
One to the Academy flew[6]
To chat among that learned crew:
Ambition moves still in his breast
That he might chant above the rest,   30
Striving for more then to do well,
That nightingales he might excell.

3 **Chief of the Brood:** Samuel, who was in England at the time
4 **second bird:** Dorothy, who with her husband, the Reverend Seaborn
Cotton, lived first in Wethersfield, Connecticut, and then in Hampton, New
Hampshire
5 **third:** Sarah, who with her husband, Richard Hubbard, lived in Ipswich
6 **One to the Academy flew:** Simon, who was a student at Harvard

5.2 Stained glass window in St. Botolph's Church, Boston, Lincolnshire, England. The image depicts Bradstreet as a mother bird, consistent with her own description in "In reference to her Children, 23. June, 1656."

ANNE BRADSTREET

My fifth,[7] whose down is yet scarce gone
Is 'mongst the shrubs and bushes flown,
And as his wings increase in strength,   35
On higher boughs he'l pearch at length.
My other three,[8] still with me nest,
Untill they'r grown, then as the rest,
Or here or there, they'l take their flight,
As is ordain'd, so shall they light.   40
If birds could weep, then would my tears
Let others know what are my fears
Lest this my brood some harm should catch,
And be surpriz'd for want of watch,
Whilst pecking corn, and void of care   45
They fall un'wares in Fowlers snare:
Or whilst on trees they sit and sing,
Some untoward boy at them do fling:
Or whilst allur'd with bell and glass,
The net be spread, and caught, alas.   50
Or least by Lime-twigs they be foyl'd,
Or by some greedy hawks be spoyl'd.
O would my young, ye saw my breast,
And knew what thoughts there sadly rest,
Great was my pain when I you bred,   55
Great was my care, when I you fed,
Long did I keep you soft and warm,
And with my wings kept off all harm,
My cares are more, and fears then ever,
My throbs such now, as 'fore were never: 60
Alas my birds, you wisdome want,
Of perils you are ignorant,
Oft times in grass, on trees, in flight,
Sore accidents on you may light.
O to your safety have an eye,   65

7 **fifth:** Dudley, who was at school in Ipswich; according to Ellis, the fifth to leave but the seventh in birth order
8 **other three:** Hannah, Mercy, and John

So happy may you live and die:
Mean while my dayes in tunes Ile spend,
Till my weak layes with me shall end.
In shady woods I'le sit and sing,
And things that past, to mind I'le bring.   70
Once young and pleasant, as are you,
But former toyes (no joyes) adieu.
My age I will not once lament,
But sing, my time so near is spent.
And from the top bough take my flight,   75
Into a country beyond sight,
Where old ones, instantly grow young,
And there with Seraphims set song:
No seasons cold, nor storms they see;
But spring lasts to eternity,   80
When each of you shall in your nest
Among your young ones take your rest,
In chirping language, oft them tell,
You had a Dam that lov'd you well,
That did what could be done for young,   85
And nurst you up till you were strong,
And 'fore she once would let you fly,
She shew'd you joy and misery;
Taught what was good, and what was ill,
What would save life, and what would kill?   90
Thus gone, amongst you I may live,
And dead, yet speak, and counsel give:
Farewel my birds, farewel adieu,
I happy am, if well with you.

A. B.

Bradstreet appears to have had an especially close relationship with her first child, Samuel, for whom she had prayed earnestly during her initially childless years of marriage. This poem expresses the same apprehension about overseas travel that she would later express about her husband's journey to England.

Upon my Son Samuel his goeing for England, Novem. 6, 1657.

Thou mighty God of Sea and Land,
I here resigne into thy hand
The Son of Prayers, of vowes, of teares,
The child I stay'd for many yeares.
Thou heard'st me then, and gav'st him me;   5
Hear me again, I give him Thee.
He's mine, but more, O Lord, thine own,
For sure thy Grace on him is shown.
No freind I have like Thee to trust,
For mortall helpes are brittle Dust.   10
Preserve, O Lord, from stormes and wrack,
Protect him there, and bring him back;
And if thou shalt spare me a space,
That I again may see his face,
Then shall I celebrate thy Praise,   15
And Blesse the for't even all my Dayes.
If otherwise I goe to Rest,
Thy Will bee done, for that is best;
Perswade my heart I shall him see
For every happefy'd with Thee.   20

Bradstreet had ample reason for apprehension about Samuel's safety during his journey to and from England. Here she describes how another ship, also sailing for England at the time, had been lost at sea. She also references the deaths by smallpox of two English royals, a brother and sister of Charles II, just before and during her son's journey.

On my Sons Return out of England, July 17, 1661.

All Praise to him who hath now turn'd
My feares to Joyes, my sighes to song,
My Teares to smiles, my sad to glad:
He's come for whom I waited long.

Thou did'st preserve him as he went;   5
In raging stormes did'st safely keep:
Did'st that ship bring to quiet Port.
The other sank low in the Deep.

From Dangers great thou did'st him free
Of Pyrates who were neer at hand;   10
And order'st so the adverse wind,
That he before them gott to Land.

In country strange thou did'st provide,
And freinds rais'd him in every Place;
And courtesies of sundry sorts   15
From such as 'fore nere saw his face.

In sicknes when he lay full sore,
His help and his Physitian wer't;
When royall ones that Time did dye,
Thou heal'dst his flesh, and cheer'd his heart.   20

From troubles and Incūmbers Thou,
Without (all fraud), did'st sett him free,

That, without scandall, he might come
To th' Land of his Nativity.

On Eagles wings him hether brought   25
Thro' Want and Dangers manifold;
And thus hath graunted my Request,
That I thy Mercyes might behold.

O help me pay my Vowes, O Lord!
That ever I may thankfull bee,   30
And may putt him in mind of what
Tho'st done for him, and so for me.

In both our hearts erect a frame
Of Duty and of Thankfullnes,
That all thy favours great receiv'd,   35
Oure upright walking may expresse.

O Lord, graunt that I may never forgett thy Loving
kindnes in this Particular, and how gratiously thou hast
answered my Desires.

Little is known about Bradstreet's mother, other than the
following epitaph.

**An Epitaph On my dear and ever honoured Mother
Mrs. Dorothy Dudley, who deceased Decemb. 27.
1643. and of her age, 61:**

Here lyes,
A Worthy Matron of unspotted life,
A loving Mother and obedient wife,

A friendly Neighbor, pitiful to poor,
Whom oft she fed, and clothed with her store;   5
To Servants wisely aweful, but yet kind,
And as they did, so they reward did find:
A true Instructer of her Family,
The which she ordered with dexterity.
The publick meetings ever did frequent,   10
And in her Closet constant hours she spent;
Religious in all her words and wayes,
Preparing still for death, till end of dayes:
Of all her Children, Children, liv'd to see,
Then dying, left a blessed memory.   15

Bradstreet's father served in various official capacities, including governor, in the fledgling Massachusetts Bay Colony. Bradstreet and others describe him as a man who was stern and proactive in his intolerance of religious aberration, a characteristic displayed during the civil trial of Anne Hutchinson. Here Bradstreet candidly describes the opposition her father sometimes met even as she celebrates his memory.

To the Memory of my dear and ever honoured Father Thomas Dudley Esq; Who deceased, July 31. 1653. and of his Age, 77.

By duty bound, and not by custome led
To celebrate the praises of the dead,
My mournfull mind, sore prest, in trembling verse
Presents my Lamentations at his Herse,
Who was my Father, Guide, Instructor too,   5
To whom I ought whatever I could doe:
Nor is't Relation near my hand shall tye;

For who more cause to boast his worth then I?
Who heard or saw, observ'd or knew him better?
Or who alive than I, a greater debtor? 10
Let malice bite, and envy knaw its fill,
He was my Father, and Ile praise him still.
Nor was his name, or life lead so obscure
That pitty might some Trumpeters procure.
Who after death might make him falsly seem 15
Such as in life, no man could justly deem.
Well known and lov'd, where ere he liv'd, by most
Both in his native, and in foreign coast,
These to the world his merits could make known,
So needs no Testimonial from his own; 20
But now or never I must pay my Sum;
While others tell his worth, I'le not be dumb:
One of thy Founders, him *New-England* know,
Who staid thy feeble sides when thou wast low,
Who spent his state, his strength, & years with care 25
That After-comers in them might have share.
True Patriot of this little Commonweal,
Who i'st can tax thee ought, but for thy zeal?
Truths friend thou wert, to errors still a foe,
Which caus'd Apostates to maligne so. 30
Thy love to true Religion e're shall shine,
My Fathers God, be God of me and mine.
Upon the earth he did not build his nest,
But as a Pilgrim, what he had, possest.
High thoughts he gave no harbour in his heart, 35
Nor honours pufft him up, when he had part:
Those titles loath'd, which some too much do love
For truly his ambition lay above.
His humble mind so lov'd humility,
He left it to his race for Legacy: 40
And oft and oft, with speeches mild and wise,
Gave his in charge, that Jewel rich to prize.
No ostentation seen in all his wayes,
As in the mean ones, of our foolish dayes,

Which all they have, and more still set to view,   45
Their greatness may be judg'd by what they shew.
His thoughts were more sublime, his actions wise,
Such vanityes he justly did despise.
Nor wonder 'twas, low things ne'r much did move
For he a Mansion had, prepar'd above,   50
For which he sigh'd and pray'd & long'd full sore
He might be cloath'd upon, for evermore.
Oft spake of death, and with a smiling chear,
He did exult his end was drawing near,
Now fully ripe, as shock of wheat that's grown,   55
Death as a Sickle hath him timely mown,
And in celestial Barn hath hous'd him high,
Where storms, nor showrs, nor ought can damnifie.
His Generation serv'd, his labours cease;
And to his Fathers gathered is in peace.   60
Ah happy Soul, 'mongst Saints and Angels blest,
Who after all his toyle, is now at rest:
His hoary head in righteousness was found:
As joy in heaven on earth let praise resound.
Forgotten never be his memory,   65
His blessing rest on his posterity:
His pious Footsteps followed by his race,
At last will bring us to that happy place
Where we with joy each others face shall see,
And parted more by death shall never be.   70

His Epitaph.

Within this Tomb a Patriot lyes
That was both pious, just and wise,
To Truth a shield, to right a Wall,
To Sectaryes a whip and Maul,
A Magazine of History,   75
A Prizer of good Company
In manners pleasant and severe

The Good him lov'd, the bad did fear,
And when his time with years was spent
If some rejoyc'd, more did lament.   80

6

SUFFERER

As a colonist, Bradstreet experienced many of the hardships afflicting the early settlers—sickness, death, and house fire—and thus was a person extremely aware of her own and her loved ones' mortality. In her poetry about suffering, she most often demonstrates a distinct pattern. First she honestly describes her feelings of loss and frustration, then she chastises herself for her attachment to earthly things or relationships, and finally she characterizes her situation as providential and beneficial for her spiritual growth.

The Bradstreets enjoyed a spacious and well-furnished house in Andover, Massachusetts, the final town in which they settled. In recounting the burning of this house on a summer night in 1666, Bradstreet reveals the stages of her struggle in coming to terms with the tragedy. She voices her distress at the loss not only of material possessions but also of the respite and fellowship the house and its contents facilitated. Chastising herself for her attachment to earthly wealth, however, she turns to God for solace and attempts to use the experience as a tool by which she might grow closer to him and anticipate her heavenly home.

Here followes some verses upon the burning of our house, July 10th, 1666. Copyed out of a loose Paper.

> In silent night when rest I took,
> For sorrow neer I did not look,
> I waken'd was with thundring nois
> And Piteous shreiks of dreadfull voice.
> That fearfull sound of fire and fire, 5
> Let no man know is my Desire.
>
> I, starting up, the light did spye,
> And to my God my heart did cry
> To strengthen me in my Distresse
> And not to leave me succourlesse. 10
> Then coming out beheld a space,
> The flame consume my dwelling place.
>
> And, when I could no longer look,
> I blest his Name that gave and took,
> That layd my goods now in the dust: 15
> Yea so it was, and so 'twas just.

6.1 The Bradstreets' new Andover house, erected on the site of their previous home, which burned July 10, 1666.

It was his own: it was not mine;
Far be it that I should repine.

He might of All justly bereft,
But yet sufficient for us left.   20
When by the Ruines oft I past,
My sorrowing eyes aside did cast,
And here and there the places spye
Where oft I sate, and long did lye.

Here stood that Trunk, and there that chest;   25
There lay that store I counted best:
My pleasant things in ashes lye,
And them behold no more shall I.
Under thy roof no guest shall sitt,
Nor at thy Table eat a bitt.   30

No pleasant tale shall 'ere be told,
Nor things recounted done of old.

143

No Candle 'ere shall shine in Thee,
Nor bridegroom's voice ere heard shall bee.
In silence ever shalt thou lye;   35
Adeiu, Adeiu; All's vanity.

Then streight I gin my heart to chide,
And did thy wealth on earth abide?
Didst fix thy hope on mouldring dust,
The arm of flesh didst make thy trust?   40
Raise up thy thoughts above the skye
That dunghill mists away may flie.

Thou hast an house on high erect
Fram'd by that mighty Architect,
With glory richly furnished,   45
Stands permanent tho' this bee fled.
It's purchased, and paid for too
By him who hath enough to doe.

A Prise so vast as is unknown,
Yet, by his Gift, is made thine own.   50
Ther's wealth enough, I need no more;
Farewell my Pelf, farewell my Store.
The world no longer let me Love,
My hope and Treasure lyes Above.

Bradstreet, typical of many colonists, struggled with various illnesses throughout her life. This record of sickness in 1632 is considered Bradstreet's earliest surviving poem and has been used by scholars to pinpoint her birthdate.

Upon a Fit of Sickness, *Anno.* 1632. Ætatis Suæ, 19.

Twice ten years old, not fully told
   Since nature gave me breath,
My race is run, my thread is spun,
   lo here is fatal Death.
All men must dye, and so must I   5
   this cannot be revok'd
For Adams sake, this word God spake
   when he so high provok'd.
Yet live I shall, this life's but small,
   in place of highest bliss,   10
Where I shall have all I can crave,
   no life is like to this.
For what's this life, but care and strife?
   since first we came from womb,
Our strength doth waste, our time doth hast,   15
   and then we go to th' Tomb.
O Bubble blast, how long can'st last?
   that always art a breaking,
No sooner blown, but dead and gone,
   ev'n as a word that's speaking.   20
O whil'st I live, this grace me give,
   I doing good may be,
Then deaths arrest I shall count best,
   because it's thy decree;
Bestow much cost there's nothing lost,   25
   to make Salvation sure,
O great's the gain, though got with pain,
   comes by profession pure.
The race is run, the field is won,
   the victory's mine I see,   30
For ever know, thou envious foe,
   the foyle belongs to thee.

Dangerous fevers were common among the early settlers. Again, Bradstreet views this distressing experience as an instrument to bring her husband and herself close to God.

For the restoration of my dear Husband from a burning Ague, June, 1661.

When feares and sorrowes me besett,
    Then did'st thou rid me out;
When heart did faint and spirits quail,
    Thou comforts me about.

Thou rais'st him up I feard to loose,   5
    Regav'st me him again:
Distempers thou didst chase away;
    With strenght didst him sustain.

My thankfull heart, with Pen record
    The Goodnes of thy God;   10
Let thy obedience testefye
    He taught thee by his rod.

And with his staffe did thee support,
    That thou by both may'st learn;
And 'twixt the good and evill way,   15
    At last, thou mig'st discern.

Praises to him who hath not left
    My Soul as destitute;
Nor turnd his ear away from me,
    But graunted hath my Suit.   20

Although Bradstreet never suffered the loss of her own infants or young children, she did experience the deaths of a number of grandchildren. In this poem about the death of her grandchild Elizabeth, the first child of her son Samuel and his wife Mercy, Bradstreet portrays the situation from a divine perspective. She hints in the first line that she had perhaps found too much earthly delight in the child. Appealing to nature imagery, she describes the child's untimely death as divinely orchestrated by God and concludes by consoling herself with the covenant belief that she will see the child again in heaven.

In memory of my dear grand-child Elizabeth Bradstreet, who deceased August, 1665. being a year and half old.

> Farewel dear babe, my hearts too much content,
> Farewel sweet babe, the pleasure of mine eye,
> Farewel fair flower that for a space was lent,
> Then ta'en away unto Eternity.
> Blest babe why should I once bewail thy fate,　　　　5
> Or sigh thy dayes so soon were terminate;
> Sith thou art setled in an Everlasting state.

2.

> By nature Trees do rot when they are grown.
> And Plumbs and Apples throughly ripe do fall,
> And Corn and grass are in their season mown,　　　　10
> And time brings down what is both strong and tall.
> But plants new set to be eradicate,

And buds new blown, to have so short a date,
Is by his hand alone that guides nature and fate.

Bradstreet also lamented the death of Samuel and Mercy's second child, Anne. Although she admits her grief, she again reminds herself of the uncertainty of earthly relationships and the certainty of reunion with the child in heaven.

In memory of my dear grand-child Anne Bradstreet. Who deceased June 20. 1669. being three years and seven Moneths old.

With troubled heart & trembling hand I write,
The Heavens have chang'd to sorrow my delight.
How oft with disappointment have I met,
When I on fading things my hopes have set?
Experience might 'fore this have made me wise,   5
To value things according to their price:
Was ever stable joy yet found below?
Or perfect bliss without mixture of woe.
I knew she was but as a withering flour,
That's here to day, perhaps gone in an hour;   10
Like as a bubble, or the brittle glass,
Or like a shadow turning as it was.
More fool then I to look on that was lent,
As if mine own, when thus impermanent.
Farewel dear child, thou ne're shall come to me,   15
But yet a while, and I shall go to thee;
Mean time my throbbing heart's chear'd up with this
Thou with thy Saviour art in endless bliss.

Here Bradstreet reflects on the death of Samuel and Mercy's fourth child, Simon. With mounting numbers of deaths, Bradstreet devotes comparatively more of this poem to forcing herself to accept "With dreadful awe" the providence of a sovereign God.

On my dear Grand-child Simon Bradstreet, Who dyed on 16. Novemb. 1669. being but a moneth, and one day old.

No sooner come, but gone, and fal'n asleep,
Acquaintance short, yet parting caus'd us weep,
Three flours, two scarcely blown, the last i'th' bud,
Cropt by th' Almighties hand; yet is he good,
With dreadful awe before him let's be mute, 5
Such was his will, but why, let's not dispute,
With humble hearts and mouths put in the dust,
Let's say he's merciful as well as just.
He will return, and make up all our losses,
And smile again, after our bitter crosses. 10
Go pretty babe, go rest with Sisters twain
Among the blest in endless joyes remain.

A. B.

Already accustomed to suffering, Anne's son Samuel endured the loss not only of four of his five children, but also of his wife, who apparently loved him deeply. Here Bradstreet again turns to nature imagery to describe untimely death, employing the metaphor of a tree with branches having been lopped off and the tree now falling to recount the deaths of Mercy's children and now Mercy herself. Throughout the poem, Bradstreet speaks directly to Samuel, who was absent on a trip to Jamaica, where he hoped his family would soon follow him. Again she finds consolation that her loved ones are at rest and asserts in her final lines that this tragic loss serves for the best in God's providence.

Anne and her husband took on the responsibility of caring for their granddaughter Mercy, the one surviving child of Samuel and Mercy. Samuel remarried in Jamaica, and after his death in 1682, his three children with his second wife were also cared for by their grandfather, Governor Bradstreet.

To the memory of my dear Daughter in Law, Mrs. Mercy Bradstreet, who deceased Sept. 6. 1669. in the 28. year of her Age.[1]

And live I still to see Relations gone,
And yet survive to sound this wailing tone;
Ah, woe is me, to write thy Funeral Song,
Who might in reason yet have lived long,
I saw the branches lopt the Tree now fall,   5
I stood so nigh, it crusht me down withal;
My bruised heart lies sobbing at the Root,
That thou dear Son hath lost both Tree and fruit:
Thou then on Seas sailing to forreign Coast;
Was ignorant what riches thou hadst lost.   10
But ah too soon those heavy tydings fly,
To strike thee with amazing misery;
Oh how I simpathize with thy sad heart,
And in thy griefs still bear a second part:

1 **Sept. 6. 1669:** an apparently incorrect date which should have been 1670, for Mercy died just after the premature birth of an infant, Anne, who was born September 3, 1670, and died soon after

I lost a daughter dear, but thou a wife,   15
Who lov'd thee more (it seem'd) then her own life.
Thou being gone, she longer could not be,
Because her Soul she'd sent along with thee.
One week she only past in pain and woe,
And then her sorrows all at once did go;   20
A Babe she left before, she soar'd above,
The fifth and last pledg of her dying love,
E're nature would, it hither did arrive,
No wonder it no longer did survive.
So with her Children four, she's now a rest,   25
All freed from grief (I trust) among the blest;
She one hath left, a joy to thee and me,
The Heavens vouchsafe she may so ever be.
Chear up, (dear Son) thy fainting bleeding heart,
In him alone, that caused all this smart;   30
What though thy strokes full sad & grievous be,
He knows it is the best for thee and me.

                        A. B.

7

SAGE

Though best known for her poetry, Bradstreet tried her hand at another genre—maxims for wise living. Similar in style, if not in content and vision of human nature, to the sayings of Benjamin Franklin, Bradstreet's collection epitomizes early American roots of wisdom.

Bradstreet used her writing as a way to offer instruction to her children, particularly near the end of her life. The following collection of wisdom, requested by her adult son Simon and contained in the leather Andover Manuscript book in Bradstreet's own writing, consists of seventy-seven aphorisms or "meditations" about life. The subjects she addresses, from childrearing to politics to spiritual growth, are as varied as those in the book of Proverbs. As she notes in her prefatory remarks, Bradstreet desired to present only original maxims, although she acknowledges that she has fallen short of this, presumably due to the universal nature of many of her observations.

For my deare sonne Simon Bradstreet.

Parents perpetuate their lives in their posterity, and their manners in their imitation. Children do natureally rather follow the failings then the vertues of their predecessors, but I am perswaded better things of you. You once desired me to leave something for you in writeing that you might look upon when you should see me no more. I could think of nothing more fit for you, nor of more ease to my self, then these short meditations following. Such as they are I bequeath to you: small legacys are accepted by true friends, much more by duty full children. I have avoyded incroaching upon others conceptions, because I would leave you nothing but myne owne, though in value they fall short of all in this kinde, yet I presume they will be better pris'd by you for the Authors sake. the Lord blesse you with grace heer, and crown you with glory heerafter, that I may meet you with rejoyceing at that great day of appearing, which is the continuall prayer, of

your affectionate mother,
March 20, 1664.   A. B.

Meditations Divine and morall.

I.

There is no object that we see; no action that we doe; no
good that we injoy; no evill that we feele, or fear, but we may
make some spirituall advantage of all: and he that makes
such improvement is wise, as well as pious.

II.

Many can speak well, but few can do well. We are better
scholars in the Theory then the practique part, but he is a
true Christian that is a proficient in both.

III.

Youth is the time of getting, middle age of improving, and
old age of spending; a negligent youth is usually attended
by an ignorant middle age, and both by an empty old age.
He that hath nothing to feed on but vanity and lyes must
needs lye down in the Bed of sorrow.

IV.

A ship that beares much saile, and little or no ballast, is easily overset; and that man, whose head hath great abilities,
and his heart little or no grace, is in danger of foundering.

V.

It is reported of the peakcock that, prideing himself in his
gay feathers, he ruffles them up; but, spying his black feet,
he soon lets fall his plumes, so he that glorys in his gifts and

7.1 Autograph letter of Anne Bradstreet to her son Simon, which serves to introduce her meditations.

but myne owne, though in value
they fall short of all in this kinde
yet I presume they will be
better pris'd by you, for the
Authors sake. the lord blesse
you wth graie heer. and Crown
you wth glory heer after. that I
may meet you wth rejoyceing
at that great day of appearing, wch is the continuall pray
er, of

your affectionate
mother : A B

March 20
1664

adornings, should look upon his Corruptions, and that will damp his high thoughts.

VI.

The finest bread hath the least bran; the purest hony, the least wax; and the sincerest christian, the least self love.

VII.

The hireling that labours all the day, comforts himself that when night comes he shall both take his rest, and receive his reward; the painfull christian that hath wrought hard in Gods vineyard, and hath born the heat and drought of the day, when he perceives his sun apace to decline, and the shadowes of his evening to be stretched out, lifts up his head with joy, knowing his refreshing is at hand.

VIII.

Downny beds make drosey persons, but hard lodging keeps the eyes open. A prosperous state makes a secure Christian, but adversity makes him Consider.

IX.

Sweet words are like hony, a little may refresh, but too much gluts the stomach.

X.

Diverse children have their different natures; some are like flesh which nothing but salt will keep from putrefaction; some again like tender fruits that are best preserved with sugar: those parents are wise that can fit their nurture according to their Nature.

XI.

That town which thousands of enemys without hath not been able to take, hath been delivered up by one traytor within; and that man, which all the temptations of Sathan without could not hurt, hath been foild by one lust within.

XII.

Authority without wisedome is like a heavy axe without an edg, fitter to bruise then polish.

XIII.

The reason why christians are so loth to exchang this world for a better, is because they have more sence then faith: they se what they injoy, they do but hope for that which is to Come.

XIV.

If we had no winter the spring would not be so pleasant: if we did not sometimes tast of adversity, prosperity would not be so welcome.

XV.

A low man can goe upright under that door, wher a taller is glad to stoop; so a man of weak faith and mean abilities, may undergo a crosse more patiently then he that excells him, both in gifts and graces.

XVI.

That house which is not often swept, makes the cleanly inhabitant soone loath it, and that heart which is not continually purifieing it self, is no fit temple for the spirit of god to dwell in.

XVII.

Few men are so humble as not to be proud of their abilitys; and nothing will abase them more then this,—What hast thou, but what thou hast received? come give an account of thy stewardship.

XVIII.

He that will untertake to climb up a steep mountain with a great burden on his back, will finde it a wearysome, if not an impossible task; so he that thinkes to mount to heaven clog'd with the Cares and riches of this Life, 'tis no wonder if he faint by the way.

XIX.

Corne, till it have past through the Mill and been ground to powder, is not fit for bread. God so deales with his servants: he grindes them with greif and pain till they turn to dust, and then are they fit manchet[1] for his Mansion.

XX.

God hath sutable comforts and supports for his children according to their severall conditions if he will make his face to

1 **manchet:** fine bread

shine upon them: he then makes them lye down in green pastures, and leades them besides the still waters;[2] if they stick in deepe mire and clay, and all his waves and billows goe over their heads, he then leads them to the Rock which is higher then they.

XXI.

He that walks among briars and thorns will be very carefull where he sets his foot. And he that passes through the wildernes of this world, had need ponder all his steps.

XXII.

Want of prudence, as well as piety, hath brought men into great inconveniencys; but he that is well stored with both, seldom is so insnared.

XXIII.

The skillfull fisher hath his severall baits for severall fish, but there is a hooke under all; Satan, that great Angler, hath his sundry baits for sundry tempers of men, which they all catch gredily at, but few perceives the hook till it be to late.

XXIV.

There is no new thing under the sun,[3] there is nothing that can be sayd or done, but either that or something like it hath been done and sayd before.

2 **makes them . . . still waters:** Ps. 23:2
3 **no new thing under the sun:** Eccl. 1:9

XXV.

An akeing head requires a soft pillow; and a drooping heart a strong support.

XXVI.

A sore finger may disquiet the whole body, but an ulcer within destroys it: so an enemy without may disturb a Commonwealth, but dissentions within over throw it.

XXVII.

It is a pleasant thing to behold the light, but sore eyes are not able to look upon it; the pure in heart shall se God, but the defiled in conscience shall rather choose to be buried under rocks and mountains then to behold the presence of the Lamb.

XXVIII.

Wisedome with an inheritance is good, but wisedome without an inheritance is better then an inheritance without wisedome.

XXIX.

Lightening doth usually preceed thunder, and stormes, raine; and stroaks do not often fall till after threat'ning.

XXX.

Yellow leaves argue want of sap, and gray haires want of moisture; so dry and saplesse performances are simptoms of little spiritall vigor.

XXXI.

Iron till it be throughly heat is uncapable to be wrought; so God sees good to cast some men into the furnace of affliction, and then beats them on his anvile into what frame he pleases.

XXXII.

Ambitious men are like hops that never rest climbing soe long as they have any thing to stay upon; but take away their props and they are, of all, the most dejected.

XXXIII.

Much Labour wearys the body, and many thoughts oppresse the minde: man aimes at profit by the one, and content in the other; but often misses of both, and findes nothing but vanity and vexation of spirit.

XXXIV.

Dimne eyes are the concomitants of old age; and short sightednes, in those that are eyes of a Republique, foretels a declineing State.

XXXV.

We read in Scripture of three sorts of Arrows,—the arrow of an enemy, the arrow of pestilence, and the arrow of a slanderous tongue; the two first kill the body, the last the good name; the two former leave a man when he is once dead, but the last mangles him in his grave.

XXXVI.

Sore labourers have hard hands, and old sinners have brawnie Consciences.

XXXVII.

Wickednes comes to its height by degrees. He that dares say of a lesse sin, is it not a little one? will ere long say of a greater, Tush, God regards it not!

XXXVIII.

Some Children are hardly weaned, although the teat be rub'd with wormwood or mustard, they wil either wipe it off, or else suck down sweet and bitter together; so is it with some Christians, let God imbitter all the sweets of this life, that so they might feed upon more substantiall food, yet they are so childishly sottish that they are still huging and sucking these empty brests, that God is forced to hedg up their way with thornes, or lay affliction on their loynes, that so they might shake hands with the world before it bid them farwell.

XXXIX.

A prudent mother will not cloth her little childe with a long and cumbersome garment; she easily foresees what events it is like to produce, at the best but falls and bruises, or perhaps somewhat worse, much more will the alwise God proportion his dispensations according to the stature and strength of the person he bestowes them on. Larg indowments of honour, wealth, or a helthfull body would quite overthrow some weak Christian, therefore God cuts their garments short, to keep them in such a trim that they might run the wayes of his Commandment.

XL.

The spring is a lively emblem of the resurrection, after a long winter we se the leavlesse trees and dry stocks (at the approach of the sun) to resume their former vigor and beauty in a more ample manner then what they lost in the Autumn; so shall it be at that great day after a long vacation, when the Sun of righteoussnes[4] shall appear, those dry bones[5] shall arise in far more glory then that which they lost at their creation, and in this transcends the spring, that their leafe shall never faile, nor their sap decline.

XLI.

A wise father will not lay a burden on a child of seven yeares old, which he knows is enough for one of twice his strength, much lesse will our heavenly father (who knowes our mould), lay such afflictions upon his weak children as would crush them to the dust, but according to the strength he will proportion the load, as God hath his little children so he hath his strong men, such as are come to a full Stature in Christ; and many times he imposes waighty burdens on their shoulders, and yet they go upright under them, but it matters not whether the load be more or lesse if God afford his help.

4 **Sun of righteoussnes:** Mal. 4:2
5 **dry bones:** Ezek. 37:1–11

XLII.

I have seen an end of all perfection (sayd the royall prophet);[6] but he never sayd, I have seen an end of all sinning: what he did say, may be easily sayd by many; but what he did not say, cannot truly be uttered by any.

XLIII.

Fire hath its force abated by water, not by wind; and anger must be alayed by cold words, and not by blustering threats.

XLIV.

A sharp appetite and a through concoction, is a signe of an healthfull body; so a quick reception, and a deliberate cogitation, argues a sound mind.

XLV.

We often se stones hang with drops, not from any innate moisture, but from a thick ayre about them; so may we sometime se marble-hearted sinners seem full of contrition; but it is not from any dew of grace within, but from some black Clouds that impends them, which produces these sweating effects.

XLVI.

The words of the wise, sath Solomon, are as nailes, and as goads,[7] both used for contrary ends,—the one holds fast, the other puts forward; such should be the precepts of the wise masters of assemblys to their heareres, not only to bid

6 **sayd the royall prophet:** Ps. 119:96
7 **as nailes, and as goads:** Eccl. 12:11

them hold fast the form of sound Doctrin, but also, so to run that they might obtain.

XLVII.

A shadow in the parching sun, and a shelter in a blustering storme, are of all seasons the most welcom; so a faithfull friend in time of adversity, is of all other most comfortable.

XLVIII.

There is nothing admits of more admiration, then Gods various dispensation of his gifts among the sons of men, betwixt whom he hath put so vast a disproportion that they scarcly seem made of the same lump, or sprung out of the loynes of one Adam; some set in the highest dignity that mortality is capable off; and some again so base, that they are viler then the earth: some so wise and learned, that they seeme like Angells among men; and some againe so ignorant and sotish, that they are more like beasts then men: some pious saints; some incarnate Devils: some exceeding beautyfull; and some extreamly deformed: some so strong and healthfull that their bones are full of marrow, and their breasts of milk; and some againe so weak and feeble, that, while they live, they are accounted among the dead,—and no other reason can be given of all this, but so it pleased him, whose will is the perfect rule of righteousnesse.

XLIX.

The treasures of this world may well be compared to huskes, for they have no kernell in them, and they that feed upon them, may soon stuffe their throats, but cannot fill their bellys; they may be choaked by them, but cannot be satisfied with them.

L.

Somtimes the sun is only shadowed by a cloud that wee cannot se his luster, although we may walk by his light, but when he is set we are in darknes till he arise again; so God doth somtime vaile his face but for a moment, that we cannot behold the light of his Countenance as at some other time, yet he affords so much light as may direct our way, that we may go forwards to the Citty of habitation, but when he seemes to set and be quite gone out of sight, then must we needs walk in darknesse and se no light, yet then must we trust in the Lord, and stay upon our God, and when the morning (which is the appointed time) is come, the Sun of righteousnes will arise with healing in his wings.

LI.

The eyes and the eares are the inlets or doores of the soule, through which innumerable objects enter, yet is not that spacious roome filled, neither doth it ever say it is enough, but like the daughters of the horsleach, crys give, give![8] and which is most strang, the more it receivs, the more empty it finds it self, and sees an impossibility, ever to be filled, but by him in whom all fullnes dwells.

LII.

Had not the wisest of men taught us this lesson, that all is vanity and vexation of spirit, yet our owne experience would

8 **crys give, give!:** Prov. 30:15

soon have speld it out; for what do we obtaine of all these things, but it is with labour and vexation? when we injoy them it is with vanity and vexation; and, if we loose them, then they are lesse then vanity and more then vexation: so that we have good cause often to repeat that sentence, vanity of vanityes, vanity of vanityes, all is vanity.[9]

LIII.

He that is to saile into a farre country, although the ship, cabbin, and provision, be all convenient and comfortable for him, yet he hath no desire to make that his place of residence, but longs to put in at that port wher his bussines lyes: a christian is sailing through this world unto his heavenly country, and heere he hath many conveniences and comforts; but he must beware of desireing to make this the place of his abode, lest he meet with such tossings that may cause him to long for shore before he sees land. We must, therfore, be heer as strangers and pilgrims, that we may plainly declare that we seek a citty above, and wait all the dayes of our appointed time till our chang shall come.

LIV.

He that never felt what it was to be sick or wounded, doth not much care for the company of the phisitian or chirurgian;[10] but if he perceive a malady that threatens him with death, he will gladly entertaine him, whom he slighted before: so he that never felt the sicknes of sin, nor the wounds of a guilty Conscience, cares not how far he keeps from him that hath skill to cure it; but when he findes his diseases to disrest him, and that he must needs perish if he have no

9 **all is vanity:** Eccl. 1:2
10 **chirurgian:** surgeon

remedy, will unfeignedly bid him welcome that brings a plaister for his sore, or a cordiall for his fainting.

LV.

We read of ten lepers[11] that were Cleansed, but of one that returned thanks: we are more ready to receive mercys then we are to acknowledg them: men can use great importunity when they are in distresses, and shew great ingratitude after their successes; but he that ordereth his conversation aright, will glorifie him that heard him in the day of his trouble.

LVI.

The remembrance of former deliverances is a great support in present destresses: he that delivered me, sath David, from the paw of the Lion and the paw of the Beare, will deliver mee from this uncircumcised Philistin;[12] and he that hath delivered mee, saith Paul, will deliver me: God is the same yesterday, to day, and for ever; we are the same that stand in need of him, today as well as yesterday, and so shall for ever.

LVII.

Great receipts call for great returnes, the more that any man is intrusted withall, the larger his accounts stands upon Gods score: it therfore behoves every man so to improve his talents,[13] that when his great master shall call him to reckoning he may receive his owne with advantage.

11 **ten lepers:** Luke 17:11–19
12 **he that delivered me, . . . Philistin:** 1 Sam. 17:37
13 **talents:** Luke 19:11–26

LVIII.

Sin and shame ever goe together. He that would be freed
from the last, must be sure to shun the company of the first.

LIX.

God doth many times both reward and punish for one and
the same action: as we see in Jehu, he is rewarded with a
kingdome to the fourth generation, for takeing veangence
on the house of Ahab;[14] and yet a little while (saith God),
and I will avenge the blood of Jezerel upon the house of
Jehu: he was rewarded for the matter, and yet punished for
the manner, which should warn him, that doth any speciall
service for God, to fixe his eye on the command, and not
on his own ends, lest he meet with Jehu's reward, which will
end in punishment.

LX.

He that would be content with a mean condition, must not
cast his eye upon one that is in a far better estate then himself, but let him look upon him that is lower then he is, and,
if he se that such a one beares poverty comfortably, it will
help to quiet him; but if that will not do, let him look on his
owne unworthynes, and that will make him say with Jacob,
I am lesse then the least of thy mercys.[15]

LXI.

Corne is produced with much labour (as the husbandman
well knowes), and some land askes much more paines then

14 **veangence on the house of Ahab:** 2 Kings 10:30
15 **least of thy mercys:** Gen. 32:10

some other doth to be brought into tilth, yet all must be ploughed and harrowed; some children (like sowre land) are of so tough and morose a disposition, that the plough of correction must make long furrows on their back, and the Harrow of discipline goe often over them, before they bee fit soile to sow the seed of morality, much lesse of grace in them. But when by prudent nurture they are brought into a fit capacity, let the seed of good instruction and exhortation be sown in the spring of their youth, and a plentifull crop may be expected in the harvest of their yeares.

LXII.

As man is called the little world, so his heart may be cal'd the little Commonwealth: his more fixed and resolved thoughts are like to inhabitants, his slight and flitting thoughts are like passengers that travell to and fro continually; here is also the great Court of justice erected, which is always kept by conscience who is both accuser, excuser, witnes, and Judg, whom no bribes can pervert, nor flattery cause to favour, but as he finds the evidence, so he absolves or condemnes: ye, so Absolute is this Court of Judicature, that there is no appeale from it,—no, not to the Court of heaven itself,—for if our conscience condemn us, he, also, who is greater then our conscience, will do it much more; but he that would have boldnes to go to the throne of grace to be accepted there, must be sure to carry a certificate from the Court of conscience, that he stands right there.

LXIII.

He that would keep a pure heart, and lead a blamlesse life, must set himself alway in the awefull presence of God, the consideration of his all-seeing eye will be a bridle to restrain from evill, and a spur to quicken on to good dutys: we certainly dream of some remotnes betwixt God and us, or else we should not so often faile in our whole Course of life as we doe; but he, that with David, sets the Lord alway in his sight, will not sinne against him.

LXIV.

We see in orchards some trees soe fruitfull, that the waight of their Burden is the breaking of their limbes; some again are but meanly loaden; and some have nothing to shew but leaves only; and some among them are dry stocks: so is it in the church, which is Gods orchard, there are some eminent Christians that are soe frequent in good dutys, that many times the waight therof impares both their bodys and estates; and there are some (and they sincere ones too) who have not attained to that fruitfullnes, altho they aime at perfection: And again there are others that have nothing to commend them but only a gay proffession, and these are but leavie christians, which are in as much danger of being cut down as the dry stock, for both cumber the ground.

LXV.

We see in the firmament there is but one Sun among a multitude of starres, and those starres also to differ much one from the other in regard of bignes and brightnes, yet all receive their light from that one Sun: so is it in the church both militant and triumphant, there is but one Christ, who is the Sun of righteousnes, in the midest of an innumerable company of Saints and Angels; those Saintes have their degrees even in this life, some are Stars of the first magnitude, and some of a lesse degree; and others (and they indeed the most in number), but small and obscure, yet all receive their luster (be it more or lesse) from that glorious sun that in-lightens all in all; and, if some of them shine so bright while they move on earth, how transcendently splendid shall they be, when they are fixt in their heavenly spheres!

LXVI.

Men that have walked very extravagantly, and at last bethink themselves of turning to God, the first thing which they eye, is how to reform their wayes rather then to beg forgivenes for their sinnes: nature lookes more at a Compensation then at a pardon; but he that will not Come for mercy without mony and without price, but bring his filthy raggs to barter for it, shall meet with miserable disapointment, going away empty, beareing the reproch of his pride and folly.

LXVII.

All the works and doings of God are wonderfull, but none more awfull then his great worke of election and Reproba-tion; when we consider how many good parents have had bad children, and againe how many bad parents have had pious children, it should make us adore the Soverainty of God, who will not be tyed to time nor place, nor yet to per-sons, but takes and chuses when and where and whom he pleases: it should alsoe teach the children of godly parents to walk with feare and trembling, lest they, through unbelief, fall short of a promise: it may also be a support to such as have or had wicked parents, that, if they abide not in un-beleif, God is able to graffe them in: the upshot of all should make us, with the Apostle, to admire the justice and mercy of God, and say, how unsearchable are his wayes, and his footsteps past finding out.[16]

16 **unsearchable . . . past finding out:** Rom. 11:33

LXVIII.

The gifts that God bestows on the sons of men, are not only abused, but most Commonly imployed for a Clean Contrary end, then that which they were given for, as health, wealth, and honour, which might be so many steps to draw men to God in consideration of his bounty towards them, but have driven them the further from him, that they are ready to say, we are lords, we will come no more at thee. If outward blessings be not as wings to help us mount upwards, they will Certainly prove Clogs and waights that will pull us lower downward.

LXIX.

All the Comforts of this life may be compared to the gourd of Jonah,[17] that notwithstanding we take great delight for a season in them, and find their shadow very comfortable, yet there is some worm or other of discontent, of feare, or greife that lyes at the root, which in great part withers the pleasure which else we should take in them; and well it is that we perceive a decay in their greennes, for were earthly comforts permanent, who would look for heavenly?

LXX.

All men are truly sayd to be tenants at will, and it may as truly be sayd, that all have a lease of their lives,—some longer, some shorter,—as it pleases our great landlord to let. All have their bounds set, over which they cannot passe, and till the expiration of that time, no dangers, no sicknes, no paines nor troubles, shall put a period to our dayes; the certainty that that time will come, together with the uncer-

17 **gourd of Jonah:** Jonah 4:6–11

tainty how, where, and when, should make us so to number our dayes as to apply our hearts to wisedome, that when wee are put out of these houses of clay,[18] we may be sure of an everlasting habitation that fades not away.

LXXI.

All weak and diseased bodys have hourly mementos of their mortality. But the soundest of men have likewise their nightly monitor by the embleam of death, which is their sleep (for so is death often calld), and not only their death, but their grave is lively represented before their eyes, by beholding their bed; the morning may mind them of the resurrection; and the sun approaching, of the appearing of the Sun of righteousnes, at whose comeing they shall all rise out of their beds, the long night shall fly away, and the day of eternity shall never end: seeing these things must be, what manner of persons ought we to be, in all good conversation?

LXXII.

As the brands of a fire, if once severed, will of themselves goe out, altho you use no other meanes to extinguish them, so distance of place, together with length of time (if there be no intercourse) will coole the affectiones of intimate friends, though there should be no displeasence betweene them.

LXXIII.

A good name is as a precious oyntment, and it is a great favour to have a good repute among good men; yet it is not that which Commends us to God, for by his ballance we

18 **houses of clay:** Job 4:19

must be weighed, and by his Judgment we must be tryed, and, as he passes the sentence, so shall we stand.

LXXIV.

Well doth the Apostle call riches deceitfull riches,[19] and they may truely be compared to deceitfull friends who speake faire, and promise much, but perform nothing, and so leave those in the lurch that most relyed on them: so is it with the wealth, honours, and pleasures of this world, which miserably delude men and make them put great confidence in them, but when death threatens, and distresse lays hold upon them, they prove like the reeds of Egipt that peirce insteed of supporting,[20] like empty wells in the time of drought, that those that go to finde water in them, return with their empty pitchers ashamed.

LXXV.

It is admirable to consider the power of faith, by which all things are (almost) possible to be done: it can remove mountaines[21] (if need were) it hath stayd the course of the sun,[22] raised the dead, cast out divels, reversed the order of nature, quenched the violence of the fire,[23] made the water become firme footing for Peter to walk on;[24] nay more then all these, it hath overcome the Omnipotent himself, as when Moses intercedes for the people,[25] God sath to him, let me alone that I may destroy them, as if Moses had been able, by the hand of faith, to hold the everlasting armes of the

19 **deceitfull riches:** 1 Tim. 6:9
20 **insteed of supporting:** 2 Kings 18:21
21 **remove mountaines:** 1 Cor. 13:2
22 **stayd the course of the sun:** Josh. 10:12–14
23 **quenched the violence of the fire:** Dan. 3
24 **water become . . . Peter to walk on:** Matt. 14:22–33
25 **Moses intercedes for the people:** Ex. 32:11–14

mighty God of Jacob; yea, Jacob himself, when he wrestled with God[26] face to face in Peniel: let me go! sath that Angell. I will not let thee go, replys Jacob, till thou blesse me! faith is not only thus potent, but it is so necessary that without faith there is no salvation, therfore, with all our seekings and gettings, let us above all seek to obtain this pearle of prise.[27]

LXXVI.

Some christians do by their lusts and Corruptions as the Isralits did by the Canaanites,[28] not destroy them, but put them under tribute, for that they could do (as they thought) with lesse hazard, and more profit; but what was the Issue? they became a snare unto them, prickes in their eyes, and thornes in their sides, and at last overcame them, and kept them under slavery: so it is most certain that those that are disobedient to the Command of God, and endeavour not to the utmost to drive out all their accursed inmates, but make a league with them, they shall at last fall into perpetuall bondage under them unlesse the great deliverer, Christ Jesus, come to their rescue.

LXXVII.

God hath by his providence so ordered, that no one Country hath all Commoditys within it self, but what it wants, another shall supply, that so there may be a mutuall Commerce through the world. As it is with Countrys so it is with men, there was never yet any one man that had all excellences, let his parts, naturall and acquired, spirituall and morall, be never so large, yet he stands in need of something

26 **wrestled with God:** Gen. 32:22–32
27 **pearle of prise:** Matt. 13:45–46
28 **the Isralits did by the Canaanites:** Josh. 16:10, 17:12–13

which another man hath, (perhaps meaner then himself,) which shews us perfection is not below, as also, that God will have us beholden one to another.

My hon^d and dear mother intended to have filled up this Book with the like observations, but was prevented by Death.[29]

---

29 **My hon^d . . . prevented by Death:** addition in Bradstreet's son Simon's handwriting

8

PILGRIM

B radstreet yearned to inculcate faith into the next generation and to encourage her children in their spiritual growth. Although her own Christian pilgrimage is reflected throughout much of her oeuvre, she outrightly chronicles it for her children's edification in the following prose and poetry.

In addition to offering the previous collection of wisdom to her children, Bradstreet also documented her own spiritual journey for them. Her son Simon, who copied Bradstreet's testament into the Andover Manuscript book, prefaces it with the following: "A true copy of a Book left by my hon'd & dear mother to her children & found among some papers after her Death."

Here Bradstreet provides a compact prose record of her early pilgrimage. In her introduction to this initial account, she displays humility by stating her goals to be her children's spiritual edification, not simply their remembrance of her when she is gone. Notably and most interesting to recent scholars, this daughter and wife of Massachusetts Bay Colony governors openly admits that as a younger person she doubted that Catholicism was altogether different from her own Protestant religion.

Following this initial account are periodic poetic and prosaic entries which continue to document Bradstreet's spiritual growth for her children. Through these entries Bradstreet demonstrates the practice of regular renewal and introspection so integral to Puritan spirituality. And she often notes the role of sickness in keeping her dependent upon God. She alternates between addressing her children and appealing to God in prayer. Some of the poetry contained in this section of the Andover Manuscript book is presented elsewhere in this volume due to its particular focus on suffering or family.

To my Dear Children.

> This Book by Any yet unread,
> I leave for you when I am dead,
> That, being gone, here you may find

What was your liveing mother's mind.
Make use of what I leave in Love   5
And God shall blesse you from above.
A. B.

My dear Children,—

I, knowing by experience that the exhortations of parents take most effect when the speakers leave to speak, and those especially sink deepest which are spoke latest—and being ignorant whether on my death bed I shall have opportunity to speak to any of you, much lesse to All—thought it the best, whilst I was able to compose some short matters, (for what else to call them I know not) and bequeath to you, that when I am no more with you, yet I may bee dayly in your remembrance, (Although that is the least in my aim in what I now doe) but that you may gain some spiritual Advantage by my experience. I have not studied in this you read to show my skill, but to declare the Truth—not to sett forth myself, but the Glory of God. If I had minded the former, it had been perhaps better pleasing to you,—but seing the last is the best, let it bee best pleasing to you.

The method I will observe shall bee this—I will begin with God's dealing with me from my childhood to this Day. In my young years, about 6 or 7 as I take it, I began to make conscience of my wayes, and what I knew was sinfull, as lying, disobedience to Parents, &c. I avoided it. If at any time I was overtaken with the like evills, it was a great Trouble. I could not be at rest 'till by prayer I had confest it unto God. I was also troubled at the neglect of Private Dutyes, tho' too often tardy that way. I also found much comfort in reading the Scriptures, especially those places I thought most concerned my Condition, and as I grew to have more understanding, so the more solace I took in them.

In a long fitt of sicknes which I had on my bed I often communed with my heart, and made my supplication to the most High who sett me free from that affliction.

But as I grew up to bee about 14 or 15 I found my heart more carnall, and sitting loose from God, vanity and the follyes of youth take hold of me.

About 16, the Lord layd his hand sore upon me and smott mee with the small pox. When I was in my affliction, I besought the Lord, and confessed my Pride and Vanity and he was entreated of me, and again restored me. But I rendered not to him according to the benefitt received.

After a short time I changed my condition and was marryed, and came into this Country, where I found a new world and new manners, at which my heart rose. But after I was convinced it was the way of God, I submitted to it and joined to the church at Boston.

After some time I fell into a lingereing sicknes like a consumption, together with a lamenesse, which correction I saw the Lord sent to humble and try me and doe mee Good: and it was not altogether ineffectuall.

It pleased God to keep me a long time without a child, which was a great greif to me, and cost mee many prayers and tears before I obtaind one, and after him gave mee many more, of whom I now take the care, that as I have brought you into the world, and with great paines, weaknes, cares, and feares brought you to this, I now travail in birth again of you till Christ bee formed in you.

Among all my experiences of God's gratious Dealings with me I have constantly observed this, that he hath never suffered me long to sitt loose from him, but by one affliction or other hath made me look home, and search what was amisse—so usually thus it hath been with me that I have no sooner felt my heart out of order, but I have expected correction for it, which most commonly hath been upon my own person, in sicknesse, weaknes, paines, sometimes on my soul, in Doubts and feares of God's displeasure, and my sincerity towards him, sometimes he hath smott a child with sicknes, sometimes chasstened by losses in estate,—and these Times (thro' his great mercy) have been the times of my greatest Getting and Advantage, yea I have found them the Times when the Lord hath manifested the most Love to me. Then have I gone to searching, and have said with David, Lord search me and try me, see what wayes of wickednes are in me, and lead me in the way everlasting:[1] and seldome or never but I have found either some sin I lay under which God would have reformed, or some duty neglected which he would have performed. And by his help I have layd Vowes and Bonds upon my Soul to perform his righteous commands.

If at any time you are chastened of God, take it as thankfully and Joyfully as in greatest mercyes, for if yee bee his yee shall reap the greatest benefitt by it. It hath been no small support to me in times of Darknes when the Almighty hath hid his face from me, that yet I have had abundance of sweetnes and refreshment after affliction, and more circumspection in my walking after I have been afflicted. I have been with God like an untoward child, that no longer then the rod has been on my back (or at least in sight) but I have been apt to forgett him and myself too. Before I was afflicted I went astray, but now I keep thy statues.

I have had great experience of God's hearing my Prayers, and returning comfortable Answers to me, either in granting the Thing I prayed for, or else in satisfying my mind without it; and I have been confident it hath been from him, because I have found my heart through his goodnes enlarged in Thankfullnes to him.

I have often been perplexed that I have not found that constant Joy in my Pilgrimage and refreshing which I sup-

1 **Lord search me . . . way everlasting:** Ps. 139:23–24

posed most of the servants of God have; although he hath not left me altogether without the wittnes of his holy spirit, who hath oft given mee his word and sett to his Seal that it shall bee well with me. I have somtimes tasted of that hidden Manna[2] that the world knowes not, and have sett up my Ebenezer,[3] and have resolved with myself that against such a promis, such tasts of sweetnes, the Gates of Hell shall never prevail. Yet have I many Times sinkings and droopings, and not enjoyed that felicity that somtimes I have done. But when I have been in darknes and seen no light, yet have I desired to stay my self upon the Lord.

And, when I have been in sicknes and pain, I have thought if the Lord would but lift up the light of his Countenance upon me, altho' he ground me to powder, it would bee but light to me; yea, oft have I thought were it hell itself, and could there find the Love of God toward me, it would bee a Heaven. And, could I have been in Heaven without the Love of God, it would have been a Hell to me; for, in Truth, it is the absence and presence of God that makes Heaven or Hell.

Many times hath Satan troubled me concerning the verity of the scriptures, many times by Atheisme how I could know whether there was a God; I never saw any miracles to confirm me, and those which I read of how did I know but they were feigned. That there is a God my Reason would soon tell me by the wondrous workes that I see, the vast frame of the Heaven and the Earth, the order of all things, night and day, Summer and Winter, Spring and Autumne, the dayly providing for this great houshold upon the Earth, the preserving and directing of All to its proper end. The consideration of these things would with amazement certainly resolve me that there is an Eternall Being.

2 **Manna:** Ex. 16
3 **Ebenezer:** 1 Sam. 7:12

But how should I know he is such a God as I worship in Trinity, and such a Saviour as I rely upon? tho' this hath thousands of Times been suggested to mee, yet God hath helped me over. I have argued thus with myself. That there is a God I see. If ever this God hath revealed himself, it must bee in his word, and this must bee it or none. Have I not found that operation by it that no humane Invention can work upon the Soul? hath not Judgments befallen Diverse who have scorned and contemd it? hath it not been preserved thro' All Ages maugre all the heathen Tyrants and all of the enemyes who have opposed it? Is there any story but that which showes the beginnings of Times, and how the world came to bee as wee see? Doe wee not know the prophecyes in it fullfilled which could not have been so long foretold by any but God himself?

When I have gott over this Block, then have I another putt in my way, That admitt this bee the true God whom wee worship, and that bee his word, yet why may not the Popish Religion bee the right? They have the same God, the same Christ, the same word: they only enterprett it one way, wee another.

This hath somtimes stuck with me, and more it would, but the vain fooleries that are in their Religion, together with their lying miracles and cruell persecutions of the Saints, which admitt were they as they terme them, yet not so to bee dealt withall.

The consideration of these things and many the like would soon turn me to my own Religion again.

But some new Troubles I have had since the world has been filled with Blasphemy, and Sectaries, and some who have been accounted sincere Christians have been carried away with them, that somtimes I have said, Is there Faith upon the earth? and I have not known what to think. But then I have remembred the words of Christ that so it must bee, and that, if it were possible, the very elect should bee deceived. Behold, saith our Saviour, I have told you before. That hath stayed my heart, and I can now say, Return, O my Soul, to thy Rest, upon this Rock Christ Jesus will I build my faith; and, if I perish, I perish. But I know all the Powers of Hell shall never prevail against it.[4] I know whom I have trusted, and whom I have beleived, and that he is able to keep that I have committed to his charge.[5]

Now to the King, Immortall, Eternall, and invisible, the only wise God, bee Honoure and Glory for ever and ever! Amen.[6]

This was written in much sicknesse and weaknes, and is very weakly and imperfectly done; but, if you can pick any Benefitt out of it, it is the marke which I aimed at.

Here follow severall occasionall meditations.

I.

By night when others soundly slept,
And had at once both ease and Rest,
My waking eyes were open kept,
And so to lye I found it best.

II.

I sought him whom my Soul did Love,   5
With tears I sought him earnestly;
He bow'd his ear down from Above,
In vain I did not seek or cry.

---

4 **upon this Rock . . . against it:** Matt. 16:18
5 **I know whom . . . to his charge:** 2 Tim. 1:12
6 **Now to the King, . . . Amen:** 1 Tim. 1:17

III.

My hungry Soul he fill'd with Good,
He in his Bottle putt my teares,[7]   10
My smarting wounds washt in his blood,
And banisht thence my Doubts and feares.

IV.

What to my Saviour shall I give,
Who freely hath done this for me?
I'le serve him here whilst I shall live,   15
And Love him to Eternity.

Meditations when my Soul hath been refreshed with the Consolations which the world knowes not.

Lord, why should I doubt any more when thou hast given me such assured Pledges of thy Love? First, thou art my Creator, I thy creature; thou my master, I thy servant. But hence arises not my comfort: Thou art my Father, I thy child. Yee shall be my Sons and Daughters, saith the Lord Almighty. Christ is my Brother; I ascend unto my Father and your Father, unto my God and your God. But least this should not bee enough, thy maker is thy husband. Nay, more, I am a member of his Body; he, my head. Such Priviledges, had not the Word of Truth made them known, who or where is the man that durst in his heart have presumed to have thought it? So wonderfull are these thoughts that my spirit failes in me at the consideration thereof; and I am confounded to think that God, who hath done so much for me, should have so little from me. But this is my comfort, when I come

7 **Bottle putt my teares:** Ps. 56:8

into Heaven, I shall understand perfectly what he hath done for me, and then shall I bee able to praise him as I ought. Lord, haveing this hope, let me purefie myself as thou art Pure, and let me bee no more affraid of Death, but even desire to bee dissolved, and bee with thee, which is best of All.

July 8th, 1656.

I had a sore fitt of fainting, which lasted 2 or 3 dayes, but not in that extremity which at first it took me, and so much the sorer it was to me because my dear husband was from home (who is my cheifest comforter on Earth); but my God, who never failed me, was not absent, but helped me, and gratiously manifested his Love to me, which I dare not passe by without Remembrance, that it may bee a support to me when I shall have occasion to read this hereafter, and to others that shall read it when I shall possesse that I now hope for, that so they may bee encourag^d to trust in him who is the only Portion of his Servants.

O Lord, let me never forgett thy Goodnes, nor question thy faithfullnes to me, for thou art my God: Thou hast said, and shall not I beleive it?

Thou hast given me a pledge of that Inheritance thou hast promised to bestow upon me. O, never let Satan prevail against me, but strenghten my faith in Thee, 'till I shall attain the end of my hopes, even the Salvation of my Soul. Come, Lord Jesus; come quickly.

> What God is like to him I serve,
>   What Saviour like to mine?
> O, never let me from thee swerve,
>   For truly I am thine.

My thankfull mouth shall speak thy praise,　　　　5
　　My Tongue shall talk of Thee:
On High my heart, O, doe thou raise,
　　For what thou'st done for me.

Goe, Worldlings, to your Vanities,
　　And heathen to your Gods;　　　　　　　　10
Let them help in Adversities,
　　And sanctefye their rods.

My God he is not like to yours,
　　Your selves shall Judges bee;
I find his Love, I know his Pow'r,　　　　　　15
　　A Succourer of mee.

He is not man that he should lye,
　　Nor son of man to unsay;
His word he plighted hath on high,
　　And I shall live for aye.　　　　　　　　20

And for his sake that faithfull is,
　　That dy'd but now doth live,
The first and last, that lives for aye,
　　Me lasting life shall give.

My soul, rejoice thou in thy God,　　　　　25
　　Boast of him all the Day,
Walk in his Law, and kisse his Rod,
　　Cleave close to him always.

What tho' thy outward Man decay,
　　Thy inward shall waxe strong;　　　　　30
Thy body vile it shall bee chang'd,
　　And glorious made ere-long.

With Angels-wings thy Soul shall mount
    To Blisse unseen by Eye,
And drink at unexhausted fount   35
    Of joy unto Eternity.

Thy teares shall All bee dryed up,
    Thy Sorrowes all shall flye;
Thy Sinns shall ne'r bee summon'd up,
    Nor come in memory.   40

Then shall I know what thou hast done
    For me, unworthy me,
And praise thee shall ev'n as I ought,
    For wonders that I see.

Base World, I trample on thy face,   45
    Thy Glory I despise,
No gain I find in ought below,
    For God hath made me wise.

Come, Jesus, quickly, Blessed Lord,
    Thy face when shall I see?   50
O let me count each hour a Day
    'Till I dissolved bee.

August 28, 1656.

After much weaknes and sicknes when my spirits were worn
out, and many times my faith weak likewise, the Lord was
pleased to uphold my drooping heart, and to manifest his
Love to me; and this is that which stayes my Soul that this
condition that I am in is the best for me, for God doth not
afflict willingly, nor take delight in greiving the children of
men: he hath no benefitt by my adversity, nor is he the better for my prosperity; but he doth it for my Advantage, and

that I may bee a Gainer by it. And if he knowes that weaknes and a frail body is the best to make me a vessell fitt for
his use, why should I not bare it, not only willingly but joyfully? The Lord knowes I dare not desire that health that
somtimes I have had, least my heart should bee drawn from
him, and sett upon the world.

Now I can wait, looking every day when my Saviour
shall call for me. Lord graunt that while I live I may doe
that service I am able in this frail Body, and bee in continuall expectation of my change, and let me never forgett
thy great Love to my soul so lately expressed, when I could
lye down and bequeath my Soul to thee, and Death seem'd
no terrible Thing. O let me ever see Thee that Art invisible, and I shall not bee unwilling to come, tho' by so rough
a Messenger.

May 11, 1657.

I had a sore sicknes, and weaknes took hold of me, which
hath by fitts lasted all this Spring till this 11 May, yet hath
my God given me many a respite, and some ability to perform the Dutyes I owe to him, and the work of my famely.

Many a refreshment have I found in this my weary Pilgrimage, and in this valley of Baca[8] many pools of water.
That which now I cheifly labour for is a contented, thankfull
heart under my affliction and weaknes, seing it is the will of
God it should bee thus. Who am I that I should repine at
his pleasure, especially seing it is for my spirituall advantage? for I hope my soul shall flourish while my body de-
cayes, and the weaknes of this outward man shall bee a
meanes to strenghten my inner man.

Yet a little while and he that shall come will come, and
will not tarry.

8 **valley of Baca:** Ps. 84:6

May 13, 1657.

As spring the winter doth succeed,
And leaves the naked Trees doe dresse,
The earth all black is cloth'd in green;
At sun-shine each their joy expresse.

My Suns returned with healing wings.   5
My Soul and Body doth rejoice;
My heart exults, and praises sings
To him that heard my wailing Voice.

My winters past, my stormes are gone,
And former clowdes seem now all fled;   10
But, if they must eclipse again,
I'le run where I was succoured.

I have a shelter from the storm,
A shadow from the fainting heat;
I have accesse unto his Throne,   15
Who is a God so wondrous great.

O hast thou made my Pilgrimage
Thus pleasant, fair, and good;
Bless'd me in Youth and elder Age,
My Baca made a springing flood?   20

I studious am what I shall doe,
To show my Duty with delight;
All I can give is but thine own,
And at the most a simple mite.

Sept. 30, 1657.

It pleased God to viset me with my old Distemper of weaknes and fainting, but not in that sore manner somtimes he

hath. I desire not only willingly, but thankfully, to submitt to him, for I trust it is out of his abundant Love to my straying Soul which in prosperity is too much in love with the world. I have found by experience I can no more live without correction then without food. Lord, with thy correction give Instruction and amendment, and then thy stroakes shall bee welcome. I have not been refined in the furnace of affliction as some have been, but have rather been preserved with sugar then brine, yet will he preserve me to his heavenly kingdom.

Thus (dear children) have yee seen the many sicknesses and weaknesses that I have passed thro' to the end that, if you meet with the like, you may have recourse to the same God who hath heard and delivered me, and will doe the like for you if you trust in him; And, when he shall deliver you out of distresse, forget not to give him thankes, but to walk more closely with him then before. This is the desire of your Loving mother,

A. B.

Just three years before her death, Bradstreet penned a poem describing her weariness of the travails of life and her desire to be with Christ. Many consider it to be the penultimate expression of the Puritan vision of life and the afterlife—surely a tempering of the Renaissance spirit of the age. Written on the final leaf of the Andover Manuscript book, it is the only poem surviving in Bradstreet's own handwriting.

"As weary pilgrim, now at rest"

> As weary pilgrim, now at rest,
>   Hugs with delight his silent nest

His wasted limbes, now lye full soft
   That myrie steps, have troden oft
Blesses himself, to think upon   5
   his dangers past, and travailes done
The burning sun no more shall heat
   Nor stormy raines, on him shall beat.
The bryars and thornes no more shall scratch
   nor hungry wolves at him shall catch   10
He erring pathes no more shall tread
   nor wild fruits eate, in stead of bread,
for waters cold he doth not long
   for thirst no more shall parch his tongue
No rugged stones his feet shall gaule   15
   nor stumps nor rocks cause him to fall
All cares and feares, he bids farwell
   and meanes in safity now to dwell.
A pilgrim I, on earth, perplext
   wth sinns wth cares and sorrows vext   20
By age and paines brought to decay
   and my Clay house mouldring away
Oh how I long to be at rest
   and soare on high among the blest.
This body shall in silence sleep   25
   Mine eyes no more shall ever weep
No fainting fits shall me assaile
   nor grinding paines my body fraile
Wth cares and fears ne'r cumbred be
   Nor losses know, nor sorrowes see   30
What tho my flesh shall there consume
   it is the bed Christ did perfume
And when a few yeares shall be gone
   this mortall shall be cloth'd upon
A Corrupt Carcasse downe it lyes   35
   a glorious body it shall rise
In weaknes and dishonour sowne
   in power 'tis rais'd by Christ alone
Then soule and body shall unite

and of their maker have the sight 40
Such lasting joyes shall there behold
    as eare ne'r heard nor tongue e'er told
Lord make me ready for that day
    then Come deare bridgrome Come away.

Aug: 31, 69.

8.1 Bradstreet's autograph.

BIBLIOGRAPHY

Writings of Anne Bradstreet

The Complete Works of Anne Bradstreet. Ed. Joseph R. McElrath Jr. and Allan P. Robb. Boston: Twayne, 1981.

Poems of Anne Bradstreet. Ed. Robert Hutchinson. New York: Dover, 1969.

The Poems of Mrs. Anne Bradstreet (1612–1672). Together with her Prose Remains with an Introduction by Charles Eliot Norton. Ed. Charles Eliot Norton. New York: Duedecimos, 1898.

The Tenth Muse Lately sprung up in America. Or, Severall Poems, compiled with great variety of Wit and Learning, full of delight. London: Stephen Bowtell, 1650.

Several Poems Compiled with great variety of Wit and Learning, full of Delight. Boston: John Foster, 1678.

The Tenth Muse (1650) and, From the Manuscripts, Meditations Divine and Morall Together with Letters and Occasional Pieces. Ed. Josephine K. Piercy. Gainesville, Fla.: Scholars' Facsimiles & Reprints, 1965.

The Works of Anne Bradstreet. Ed. Jeannine Hensley. Cambridge, Mass.: Belknap Press of Harvard University Press, 1967.

The Works of Anne Bradstreet in Prose and Verse. Ed. John Harvard Ellis. Charlestown, Mass.: A. E. Cutter, 1867. Gloucester, Mass.: Peter Smith, 1932, 1962.

Other Sources

Bercovitch, Sacvan. *The Puritan Origins of the American Self*. New Haven: Yale University Press, 1975.

Berryman, John. *Homage to Mistress Bradstreet*. New York: Farrar, Straus & Co., 1956.

Bremer, Francis J. *John Winthrop: America's Forgotten Founding Father.* Oxford: Oxford University Press, 2003.

Dickens, A. G. *The English Reformation.* 2nd ed. University Park: The Pennsylvania State University Press, 1989.

Doriani, Beth M. "'Then Have I . . . Said With David': Anne Bradstreet's Andover Manuscript Poems and the Influence of the Psalm Tradition." *Early American Literature* 24 (1989): 52–69.

Eberwein, Jane Donahue. "Civil War and Bradstreet's 'Monarchies.'" *Early American Literature* 26 (1991): 119–44.

———. "'No Rhet'ric We Expect': Argumentation in Bradstreet's 'The Prologue.'" *Early American Literature* 16 (1981): 19–26.

———. "The 'Unrefined Ore' of Anne Bradstreet's Quaternions." *Early American Literature* 9 (1974): 19–26.

Gordon, Charlott. *Mistress Bradstreet: The Untold Life of America's First Poet.* New York: Little, Brown and Company, 2005.

Hambrick-Stowe, Charles E., ed. *Early New England Meditative Poetry: Anne Bradstreet and Edward Taylor.* New York: Paulist, 1988.

Hammond, Jeffrey A. *Sinful Self, Saintly Self: The Puritan Experience of Poetry.* Athens, Ga.: University of Georgia Press, 1993.

Knight, Janice. *Orthodoxies in Massachusetts: Rereading American Puritanism.* Cambridge, Mass.: Harvard University Press, 1994.

Kopacz, Paula. "'To Finish What's Begun': Anne Bradstreet's Last Words." *Early American Literature* 23 (1988): 175–87.

Margerum, Eileen. "Anne Bradstreet's Public Poetry and the Tradition of Humility." *Early American Literature* 17 (1982): 152–60.

Martin, Wendy. *An American Triptych: Anne Bradstreet, Emily Dickinson, Adrienne Rich.* Chapel Hill: University of North Carolina Press, 1984.

Mather, Cotton. *Magnalia Christi Americana, Books I and II.* Ed. Kenneth B. Murdock. Cambridge, Mass.: Belknap Press of Harvard University Press, 1977.

Meserole, Harrison T., ed. *American Poetry of the Seventeenth Century.* University Park: The Pennsylvania State University Press, 1985.

Miller, Perry. *The American Puritans: Their Prose and Poetry.* Garden City, NY: Doubleday, 1956.

———. *Errand Into the Wilderness.* Cambridge, Mass.: Belknap Press of Harvard University Press, 1956.

Piercy, Josephine K. *Anne Bradstreet.* New Haven: College and University Press, 1965.

Requa, Kenneth A. "Anne Bradstreet's Poetic Voices." *Early American Literature* 9 (1974): 3–18.

Rosenmeier, Rosamond. *Anne Bradstreet Revisited.* Boston: Twayne, 1991.

Ryken, Leland. *Worldly Saints: The Puritans As They Really Were.* Grand Rapids: Academie Books, 1986.

Salska, Agnieszka. "Puritan Poetry: Its Public and Private Strain." *Early American Literature* 19 (1984): 107–21.

Scheick, William J. *Design in Puritan American Literature.* Lexington: The University Press of Kentucky, 1992.

Schweitzer, Ivy. "Anne Bradstreet Wrestles with the Renaissance." *Early American Literature* 23 (1988): 291–312.

Stanford, Ann. "Anne Bradstreet: Dogmatist and Rebel." *Critical Essays on Anne Bradstreet.* Ed. Pattie Cowell and Ann Stanford. Boston: Hall, 1983. 76–88.

Taylor, Edward. *Edward Taylor's* Gods Determinations *and* Preparatory Meditations. Ed. Daniel Patterson. Kent, Ohio: The Kent State University Press, 2003.

White, Elizabeth Wade. *Anne Bradstreet: "The Tenth Muse."* New York: Oxford University Press, 1971.

Winthrop, John. *The Journal of John Winthrop, 1630–1649.* Ed. Richard S. Dunn and Laetitia Yeandle. Abr. ed. Cambridge, Mass.: Belknap Press of Harvard University Press, 1996.

Wright, Nancy E. "Epitaphic Conventions and the Reception of Anne Bradstreet's Public Voice." *Early American Literature* 31 (1996): 243–62.

ABOUT THE ILLUSTRATIONS

Portrait of James I. From *A History of the American People*, by Woodrow Wilson, Vol. 1. New York and London: Harper & Brothers Publishers, 1906. "Portrait and autograph of James I. From a painting by C. Johnson, in the possession of W. J. Hay, at Duns, England."

Portrait of John Cotton. From *A History of the American People*, by Woodrow Wilson, Vol. 1. New York and London: Harper & Brothers Publishers, 1906. "Portrait and autograph of John Cotton. From the original painting owned by his descendant, Miss Adele G. Thayer, of Brookline, Mass."

Portrait of Charles I. From *A History of the American People*, by Woodrow Wilson, Vol. 1. New York and London: Harper & Brothers Publishers, 1906. "Portrait and autograph of Charles I. From an engraving after the painting by Sir Anthony Vandyck."

Early Map of Boston Harbor. From *Boston: The Place and the People*, by M. A. DeWolfe Howe. Illustrated by Louis A. Holman. New York: The Macmillan Company, 1903. "Earliest chart of Boston Harbor."

Arrival of John Winthrop's company in Boston Harbor. From *A History of the American People*, by Woodrow

Wilson, Vol. 1. New York and London: Harper & Brothers Publishers, 1906. "Arrival of Winthrop's company in Boston Harbor. From the painting by William Formby Halsall, in the possession of Walter B. Ellis, Esq., of Boston, Mass."

Portrait of John Winthrop. From *Boston: The Place and the People*, by M. A. DeWolfe Howe. Illustrated by Louis A. Holman. New York: The Macmillan Company, 1903. "John Winthrop: autograph, seal, and portrait by Van Dyck, in Massachusetts State House."

Initial word of Massachusetts Bay Colony charter. From *Boston: The Place and the People*, by M. A. DeWolfe Howe. Illustrated by Louis A. Holman. New York: The Macmillan Company, 1903. "Initial, original charter, Massachusetts Bay Company."

Anne Hutchinson preaching. From *A History of the American People*, by Woodrow Wilson, Vol. 1. New York and London: Harper & Brothers Publishers, 1906. "Anne Hutchinson preaching in her house in Boston. From a painting by Howard Pyle."

Title page of 1650 edition of *The Tenth Muse*. From *An Account of Anne Bradstreet: The Puritan Poetess and Kindred Topics*, edited by Colonel Luther Caldwell. Boston: Damrell & Upham, 1898. "Title page, first edition, London, 1650 *The Tenth Muse*."

Title page of 1678 edition of *The Tenth Muse*. Courtesy of the Rare Book Division of the Library of Congress.

Portrait of Sir Walter Raleigh. From *Sir Walter Raleigh: A Biography*, by William Stebbing. Oxford: Clarendon Press, 1891. "From the Duke of Rutland's Miniature."

***Bay Psalm Book* title page.** From *A History of the American People*, by Woodrow Wilson, Vol. 1. New York and London: Harper & Brothers Publishers, 1906. "Title page of the *Bay Psalm Book*. Facsimile of the first edition from the Lenox copy in New York Public Library. Altogether ten copies are known of this first book printed in English America, by Stephen Day, or Daye, at Cambridge, Mass. For the latest account of its history and seventeenth century editions, see *The Literary Collector*, vol. iii (1901), 69–72."

***Day of Doom* title page.** From *American Lands and Letters: The Mayflower to Rip Van Winkle*, by Donald G. Mitchell. New York: Charles Scribner's Sons, 1897. "Title page of *The Day of Doom*. From a copy at the Lenox Library."

***The Simple Cobbler* title page.** From *American Lands and Letters: The Mayflower to Rip Van Winkle*, by Donald G. Mitchell. New York: Charles Scribner's Sons, 1897. "Title page of *The Simple Cobbler of Aggawamm*. From a copy in possession of the author."

Elizabeth I signature. From *A History of the American People*, by Woodrow Wilson, Vol. 1. New York and London: Harper & Brothers Publishers, 1906. "Autograph of Queen Elizabeth. Much reduced in size."

Portrait of Simon Bradstreet. From *An Account of Anne Bradstreet: The Puritan Poetess and Kindred Topics*, edited by Colonel Luther Caldwell. Boston: Damrell & Upham, 1898. "Governor Simon Bradstreet."

Stained glass window in St. Botolph's Church. By kind permission of the Vicar and Churchwardens of St. Botolph's Church, Boston, England.

Andover house. From *An Account of Anne Bradstreet: The Puritan Poetess and Kindred Topics*, edited by Colonel Luther Caldwell. Boston: Damrell & Upham, 1898. "Andover House: Gen. Bradstreet's and Anne Bradstreet's home at North Andover, erected on the site of the one burned on July 10, 1666."

Handwritten letter to Bradstreet's son Simon. From *An Account of Anne Bradstreet: The Puritan Poetess and Kindred Topics*, edited by Colonel Luther Caldwell. Boston: Damrell & Upham, 1898. "Autograph letter of Anne Bradstreet."

Bradstreet's signature. From *An Account of Anne Bradstreet: The Puritan Poetess and Kindred Topics*, edited by Colonel Luther Caldwell. Boston: Damrell & Upham, 1898. "Autograph signature of Anne Bradstreet."

INDEX OF PERSONS

INDEX OF BRADSTREET'S WORKS

Heidi L. Nichols (M.A. Villanova University, Ph.D. Indiana University of Pennsylvania) is assistant professor of English at Lancaster Bible College. She is the author of *The Fashioning of Middle-Class America: Sartain's Union Magazine of Literature and Art and Antebellum America*.